Cultural Attitudes

Marie-Louise von Franz, Honorary Patron

**Studies in Jungian Psychology
by Jungian Analysts**

Daryl Sharp, General Editor

Cultural Attitudes
in Psychological Perspective

Joseph L. Henderson, M.D.

INNER CITY
BOOKS

Canadian Cataloguing in Publication Data

Henderson, Joseph L. (Joseph Lewis), 1903-
   Cultural attitudes in psychological perspective

(Studies in Jungian psychology by Jungian analysts; 19

Bibliography: p.
Includes index.

ISBN 0-919123-18-X

1. Attitude (Psychology). 2. Cultural relativism—
Psychological aspects. 3. Individuation.
4. Jung, C. G. (Carl Gustav), 1875-1961. I. Title.
II. Series.

BF378.A75H45 1984   152.4′52   C84-099208-4

INNER CITY BOOKS
Box 1271, Station Q, Toronto, Canada M4T 2P4
Telephone (416) 927-0355

Honorary Patron: Marie-Louise von Franz.
Publisher and General Editor: Daryl Sharp.
Editorial Board: Fraser Boa, Daryl Sharp, Marion Woodman.

INNER CITY BOOKS was founded in 1980 to promote the
understanding and practical application of the work of C.G. Jung.

Cover: Nature Overshadows All (1983), three-dimensional optical
orphan (sparkle, glass, silicone, enameled steel) by Canadian artist
Jerry Pethick. (Publisher's Collection)

Glossary and Index by Daryl Sharp.

Printed and bound in Canada by Webcom Limited

Contents

Acknowledgments   6
Introduction   7

PART ONE: FOUR CULTURAL ATTITUDES

1 The Social Attitude   17
2 The Religious Attitude   27
3 The Aesthetic Attitude   45
4 The Philosophic Attitude   59
5 Discussion of the Cultural Attitudes   72

PART TWO: A PSYCHOLOGICAL ATTITUDE

6 Dualities of the Self   81
7 Psychology in Historical Context   88
8 Psychology in Its Modern Context   93
9 Nature and Psyche   98

Notes   107
Glossary of Jungian Terms   113
Bibliography   115
Index   120

See final pages for descriptions of other Inner City Books

Acknowledgments

I am indebted to Professor Jung for helpful encouragement at the outset of my research, and to M. Esther Harding and Edward Edinger, who criticized and helped clarify it at a later date. The initial study of culture in respect to analytical psychology was made possible by a grant from the Bollingen Foundation in 1963.

An outline of my research on cultural attitudes appears in "The Archetype of Culture," a paper delivered in 1962 at the Second International Congress of Analytical Psychologists in Zurich. Further lectures on this subject were presented at the IAAP Congress of 1974 in London, and at the First Panarion Conference in Los Angeles in 1975. "Individuals in a Changing Society" is a paper on this subject which was published in *Psychological Perspectives* in 1977.

Introduction

It has often been suggested that psychology might have a place of its own in the spectrum of cultural attitudes, and in this work I have used my experience as a psychotherapist to describe what I think this attitude is and how it functions. We need to show how the growth of psychological awareness may rescue certain individuals from an unconscious identity with other cultural attitudes. Moreover, the psychological attitude of which I am thinking enables people to become acquainted with other cultural attitudes in a new way and to view themselves with greater cultural objectivity. I believe that psychological insight of this kind need not separate us from the genuine influence of culture, though psychological analysis is lethal to stereotyped traditions preserved by the inertia of pure habit.

There is a possible objection to considering that psychology can be regarded as a cultural attitude in its own right, if we think we should offer a completely uniform theory by which to represent it. Such uniformity as this seems to entail would not be psychologically desirable, even if it were possible. Freudians have to remain Freudians, Jungians Jungians and so it is with other psychological schools. Existentialist analysts commendably tried to correct this exclusive identification with "schools" and urged their followers to move freely from one discipline to another, not defining themselves as belonging to any school. Even so, they did not avoid the widespread group identification which ultimately crystallized into the Human Potential Movement of the sixties and seventies, with its holistic values but also its prejudices. Hence we cannot eliminate differences of psychological opinion, but rather welcome them and enjoy their ferment.

The Jungian individuation process provides the model for my demonstration of psychological development, and it may be argued that an attitude based on individuation alone sets an impossibly high goal. If so, I should like to correct this opinion. Individuation is not a form of elitism. That could only apply to some sterile secret order or cult, like the group of men in Hermann Hesse's novel, *The Glassbead Game*, in which an intellectual number-game becomes the sole occupation of all those chosen spirits capable of playing it. Quite appropriately Hesse shows the ultimate disillusionment of his hero, Knecht, who leaves the group because it has no connection with ordinary life or with contemporary culture. It is precisely in this sense that a true psychological attitude may come into being in order to preserve the balance between the culture and the need of any one vitally interested, conscious individual, as I show later in my interpretation of a woman's dream in which she had to weed her vegetables on a collective farm.

Throughout history we find that certain cultural traditions vanish or are suspended as if they no longer existed. One could point to the decade following World War I as a time during which the traditional cultural values were thus disturbed. In 1927 Jung voiced his concern as follows: "Everywhere one hears the cry for a *Weltanschauung*; everyone asks the meaning of life and the world."[1]

Weltanschauung is an untranslatable word which Jung describes as having "much in common with an attitude. . . . that has been formulated into concepts."[2] The loss of such attitudes leads therefore to a loss of cultural identity and brings a feeling of demoralization. This leaves certain individuals or even whole groups without their accustomed creative work to perform or even the opportunity to collaborate in the change of the cultural canon of their time. It is significant that it was during this period of the 1920s that depth psychology, spearheaded by Freudian psychoanalysis, had its strongest initial influence upon culture as a whole. Does this mean that a psychological attitude comes into being only when one of the major cultural attitudes fails?

There is a good deal of evidence to think this may still be so during our current period of history in which, for instance, the failure of organized religion to meet the spiritual needs of larger and larger numbers of people is being compensated by an increased psychological interest even among the clergy, many of whom now use psychotherapy or psychological counseling. Also many members of the clergy themselves are personally finding the psychological individuation process a factor which was always implicit in the best religious leaders. Similarly, other people with a predominant social attitude may experience disillusionment with the soulless nature of politics and rescue themselves by learning to understand the psychology of power so as to separate themselves from its baneful influence.

For example, in the seventeenth century a brilliant group of aristocrats, i.e., Duc de la Rochefoucauld, Duc de Saint-Simon, Mme de Lafayette and Mme de Sévigné, created an aphoristic and biographical literature which is remarkably modern in its perception of the real springs of human motivation and the psychology of power politics. Again in the nineteenth century Stendhal provided a similar critique in his psychological novels and this tradition was well tended by Flaubert, Anatole France, Zola and Proust. Such activity has made of French literature a strong social force at the same time that it has achieved a high degree of psychological awareness.

Also, in times of change an aesthetic or philosophic attitude may be revived where religious or social attitudes fail, and we cannot therefore claim that a psychological attitude per se provides the only cure for all cultural failures. In many cases a shift from one attitude to another carries many people in the surprising twists and turns of the spirit of their time. Here Jung advised caution in believing that his analytical psychology was itself a *Weltanschauung*. It cannot take the place of a traditional cultural attitude, but can, however, add something to it. Jung says:

> If, therefore, I had to name the most essential thing that analytical psychology can add to our *Weltanschauung*, I should say it is the recognition that there exist certain unconscious contents which make demands that cannot be denied, or send forth influences with which the conscious mind must come to terms, whether it will or not.[3]

Jung himself did not try to formulate the cultural changes which may affect the *Weltanschauung* nor did he describe how it "has been formulated into concepts." But his follower, Erich Neumann, provides an excellent example of cultural change and has illustrated this by means of diagrams showing how the cultural canon was affected by individual variants in the rise and development of art in the Christian era.[4] This type of study confirms Jung's observations:

> *Weltanschauung* embraces all sorts of attitudes to the world, including the philosophical. Thus there is an aesthetic, a religious, an

idealistic, a realistic, a romantic, a practical *Weltanschauung*, to mention only a few possibilities.[5]

There are today, however, an increasing number of people who find in psychology a new point of view which need not criticize, supplant or rescue its possessor from cultural lapses but which exists in its own right, and they have some tradition for this. They become psychologists in the best sense, men such as William James whose unfailing interest in people and the human condition allows them to synthesize many different points of view in creating that aspect of philosophy which can only be called *psychology* (knowledge of the psyche) because of its immediate concern with the practical problems of living. James's *Pragmatism, A New Name For Some Old Ways of Thinking*, growing out of Josiah Royce's highly introverted social philosophy, established a new and very American form of psychological attitude. In order to understand it we need not have recourse to any religious belief, nor ethical system, nor social standard, nor aesthetic principle. It stands on its own while at the same time maintaining a lively relationship with culture as a whole.

James says of pragmatism:

> Against rationalism as a pretension and a method pragmatism is fully armed and militant. But, at the outset, at least, it stands for no particular results. It has no dogmas, and no doctrines save its method. As the young Italian pragmatist Papini has well said, it lies in the midst of our theories, like a corridor in a hotel. Innumerable chambers open out of it. In one you may find a man writing an aesthetic volume; in the next someone on his knees praying for faith and strength; in a third a chemist investigating a body's properties. In a fourth a system of idealistic metaphysics is being excogitated; in a fifth the impossibility of metaphysics is being shown. But they all own the corridor, and all must pass through it if they want a practicable way of getting into or out of their respective rooms.[6]

In response to pragmatism a variety of psychological attitudes emerged into the twentieth century, and some people are presumably still content with this tradition. But for many more, in the light of the development of depth psychology, this was not enough, and a change has taken place. As long as psychology was only "pragmatic," it was identical with a belief in the primary nature of the conscious will. Freud's contribution changed all this and his followers were convinced of the primary nature of the unconscious, which quickly created a viewpoint in conflict with the previous one.

Jung introduced a principle of relativity into this apparent opposition and reformulated both tendencies as a reversible complementarity between the conscious and the unconscious, which he felt was inherent in all psychic functioning. The ego then experiences an enlargement of its field of vision so that an interaction between these two, where one is thesis and the other is antithesis, results in a new synthesis. When this happens ego-consciousness is necessarily displaced from its role as observer of consciousness and becomes equally an observer of the unconscious; this cannot be a scientifically dispassionate observation, however, but that of a participant-observer who is affected by and changed in the process.

Our laboratory for studying this process is found in analysis or psychotherapy of a depth appropriate to expose the formative nature of the unconscious. We may experience it in the interpersonal relationship of analyst and patient, in working through the transference of the patient and the countertransference of the analyst which imply a mutual projection of unconscious factors. Usually this has been discussed by analysts either as a very personal experience, revealing a psychosexual attraction-repulsion syndrome, or else it is seen in the fascination both patient and doctor experience for certain archetypal patterns emerging from the collective unconscious in the dreams or fantasies of the patient.

But there is another element in transference, and especially in the analyst's countertransference, that arises from differences in cultural identity between analyst and patient. I call these cultural attitudes the social, the religious, the aesthetic and the philosophic. In recognizing and accepting a transference from my patients or my countertransference to them, I have found it important to determine the nature of the patient's strongest cultural attitude and the response I may have to it from my own dominant cultural attitude. If we have both developed the same cultural attitudes we may seem to enjoy a comfortable sense of agreement. But this can be misleading and may prevent us from getting down to work at the basic psychological problem. We may just intensify our own blind spots. On the other hand, if our cultural attitudes are too different we may meet unexpected resistances and make mutually negative projections upon each other. So the analyst may easily experience both positive and negative forms of countertransference here.

I could cite many instances where cultural attitudes have influenced the countertransference but will content myself with two brief examples. The first is an experience of mine, when I caught myself in a state of positive countertransference to a patient because of his cultural identity. This was a man with a well-developed philosophic attitude and a facility of language that expressed it with great clarity. I looked forward to our sessions as eagerly as if I were a student in an interesting doctoral program. I only realized the nature of the countertransference when he rather abruptly terminated his therapy and wrote a book instead. I had to nurse my disappointment for some time until I realized how much I had expected him to profit from my investment of interest in him. I then discovered that a large part of my interest was illusory since his philosophic attitude, as he expounded it in his book, did not interest me in any lasting sense. I have had similar experiences with people through whose cultural attitudes I unconsciously gained support for my own. And so I have found that however valid it may be to learn from one's patients, it is also necessary to let them go into the next period of their lives without fulfilling one's own therapeutic program for their cultural development, however alluring it may be. This is the essence of the self-analysis of the countertransference. Needless to say, if one does try to force a recognition of one's own cultural attitude when it is at variance with that of the patient, the patient will either become unaccountably resistant or change analysts. This brings me to my second example.

A colleague of mine was in a period of his life where a social attitude had become dominant over a previous religious attitude which had been part of his natural heritage. He had become convinced that it is our duty to react to political and social injustice by word and deed at all times to correct any kind of bigotry. This was a valid stage in his own development, but it was not always right for his patients. One of his patients was a reflective man with an aesthetic attitude who ignored social issues as much as possible. He was a photographer and filmmaker interested primarily in form and design, only secondarily in content. The analyst could not restrain himself from criticizing this attitude and for expecting to arouse his patient's interest in social welfare as a corrective for what seemed to him mere narcissism. The patient tried at first to satisfy his analyst's expectations of him, but instead of helping him it drove him into even greater neurotic conflict than he had experienced before. At length he left his analyst and came to me with his sad story of social defeat. As soon as he got from me an acknowledgment that there is a healthy cultural aesthetic attitude, which needs no social justification for its existence, his resistance vanished and his therapy went forward. In the end it actually enabled him to criticize and to a large extent separate himself from what were in fact somewhat narcissistic overtones in his aesthetic attitude and to promote his interests with more vigor, and it led to greater success in his career. Paradoxically, it did lead to an increased awareness of social issues but not to a greater sense of social responsibility. His duty remained with his art.

I have sometimes responded to a patient's religious attitude when it is strongly marked and very different from my own. If this countertransference is positive I may be drawn into believing that the analysis really is a religious experience, or at least a sort of spiritual exercise. This tendency is especially marked in Jungian analysis because Jung himself emphasized the religious value of the individuation process, and many religious people are drawn to this type of therapy for that very reason. Experience has taught me to watch out for this attempt to draw me into accepting uncritically a patient's religious belief-system instead of defending my own psychological point of view, not because I am opposed to his or her religious attitude but in order to bring out what is unconscious in it.

I often have great difficulty with my patients and with myself in learning to adjust the religious nature of our work so as to honor its symbolic content without embracing any particular dogma. In so doing I am forced to define and redefine a psychological attitude as a value in its own right. Jung himself has many times redefined the religious attitude, which Daryl Sharp describes as

> an attitude of mind based on an experience of transcendental reality, *the reality of the psyche*. With this goes an attitude that acknowledges the presence of autonomous gods within, in other words archetypal contents to which the ego itself is subordinate and must pay heed.[7]

When I am drawn into acknowledging the validity of a dominant cultural attitude in my patients, or when they feel I do not understand them because I do not have as perfect an attitude as their social or religious or aesthetic or philosophic attitude, I must try not to fall into this trap, but convince them as tactfully as possible that my cultural attitude is by now dominantly psychological. In so doing I may enable them to take from my psychological attitude something to enrich and profitably modify their own. This will be discussed further after exploring some examples of the traditional cultural attitudes.

PART ONE

FOUR CULTURAL ATTITUDES

Frontispiece of *Leviathan* by Thomas Hobbes.

1

The Social Attitude

Influenced as we are today by the claims of countercultural movements, I often have to ask myself what my role is expected to be for each individual patient in my care. What social trend is he identified with, and in which direction is he moving? How am I affected by these trends? To what extent am I vulnerable? Naturally, I have no definitive answer to such questions, but empirically, I try to rely upon my own social attitude so as not to become confused by contrasting pressures. This, of course, eliminates xenophobic people, those unduly fearful of other views, since they can only be treated symptomatically by their peers for whatever identity crisis occurs in relation to the group itself. Only if allegiance to the group becomes relative to the need for a special, individual self-definition can the necessary dialogue take place between the individual and the group.

In the initial state of such an analysis I may then have to decide whether my patient is identified with a stable group or whether he or she is in a transitional state. Actually there are no absolutely stable groups since every society, as the social anthropologist Victor Turner has shown in his study of African tribes, contains within it a minority group that can be regarded as liminal to the establishment but which influences it from within. If my patient is in such a transitional state I may be called upon to help him "to enter into a dialogue with structure."[8] When this is successful I have helped him achieve a new kind of social identity. But it may happen the other way around, where my patient has a well-structured social attitude, in relation to which I am in a liminal position. In earlier years, indeed, I had to reckon with my own inadequacy as a judge for any social attitude, since it was my least developed attitude in boyhood and my respect for its validity was slow in coming.

The social attitude, generally speaking, is concerned with maintaining the ethical code of the culture, whether of the established culture or any specific countercultural deviation from it. I have often found this attitude provides a particular resistance to analysis, since the patient may assume that if the social problems of our time were solved, all conflict would vanish and psychotherapy would be unnecessary. At this point I have had to be careful not to allow my own social attitude, when it differed from that of my patients, to dominate or suppress their own. But I have had to let them know that any true social attitude is not to be confused with political opinions or social fashions of behavior. This is the point at which an understanding of the individuation process is necessary on the part of the therapist in order to avoid wasting time with discussions of worldly adaptations or with conflicting partisan viewpoints.

A knowledge of individuation persuades us that in any true study of social consciousness we cannot resort to the usual criteria for classifying responses, since we are concerned with the subjective as well as objective nature of individual reactions, including our own. We are, therefore, more concerned with what occurs by significant correspondence of one thing with another, than by serial causation. From the ancient Chinese *Art of the Mind* there is a saying which expresses this method as follows:

> What man desires to know is *that* (i.e., the external world). But his means of knowing it is *this* (i.e., himself). How can he know *that*? Only by the perfection of *this*.[9]

It is occasionally said that depth analysis promotes an autonomy of the individual at the expense of his social adaptation. In relation to politics, this is often true. A stage of individualism, even selfishness, is inevitable at the beginning of any process of self-discovery in order to break one's original identity with the class into which one has been born, or the kind of family identity that keeps us unconscious. If, however, the individualism of this first break with tradition becomes fixed, its narcissistic eccentricity precludes any truly social attitude. The kind of psychological development we see during a sufficiently long period of analysis convinces me that there must come a time for a reacceptance of the social dimension of life in the process of individuation itself. This is not like the previous unconscious identification with a particular class or belief-system but is born in response to an individual need.

A woman in her late forties who had had a very strong sense of social identity, in accordance with her highly effective extraverted personality, withdrew more and more into herself during the first part of her analysis. She accordingly became individualistic in the sense I have described. The value of this experience lay in the entirely legitimate, and even necessary, development of religious and philosophic attitudes which gave new depth and inner meaning to a life which might otherwise have wasted its talents in ambitiously but blindly "doing good." But the growing exclusiveness of her new attitude of self-collection limited her so much that she became somewhat isolated from the world. Her problem at this time seemed to me typical of certain analysands, and of all those who chase after introverted cult practices. They find so much interest in pursuing further knowledge of the inner meaning of life that any need for involvement in the affairs of a specific social community is virtually forgotten. At the point when she was ready to change this pattern she had the following dream:

> I saw tuberous edible vegetables growing in rows in the midst of thick grass on a collective farm. With more decentralization of the commune there could be better cultivation and the plants could be freed from the grass. There is too much bureaucracy.

The dream was accompanied by a drawing of one of these vegetables. It was shaped like a summer squash, round with scalloped edges and a convex center. There arose from a hole in the exact center some tall stalks looking rather like several stamens of a flower. The vegetable was attached to the ground by an intricate root system, which, as she described it, was surrounded and overgrown with grass.

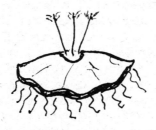

Though the vegetable represented a conservatism which had allowed her inwardly to achieve a new sense of rootedness and a sense of wholeness, she had turned too far away from her actual social connections. The vegetable is not only representative of a conservative introverted tendency toward self-definition, however. The outgoing, in her case, intuitive quality of her personality is still there in the central stalk, which becomes now a symbol of that which can transcend the passivity of the resting phase of the cycle of life. But her precious vegetable is in a field with others and in danger of being choked by weeds, if she does not recultivate it with a new awareness of the need for meaningful separateness from the other plants in the same field. This field evokes a social pattern as far from her conscious way of life as would be possible to imagine—a collective farm in a communist state. Apparently just such a social image was required to compensate her psychological individualism.

This case seems to show that when an important cultural attitude is neglected, first it is the individual who suffers. In this case her individual life needed weeding, while her social identity suffered from having become blindly collectivized. Indeed, any social organization, whether it is a communist state or a capitalist democracy, becomes ineffective only when it is depersonalized (bureaucratic) and overcrowded. This woman had become conservatively individual at the expense of a social attitude which had in turn reverted to an overly programmed social pattern where no individual can flourish adequately. The cure lay in becoming once more socially oriented outwardly in accordance with her growing sense of true individuality with its social viability.

This case also shows the importance of honoring the feminine point of view in a very practical way. What is involved here is not a traditionally masculine idealism pointing the way to a social utopia, but a more immediate, essentially feminine, social experiment. In this sense women perform social duties with a special ability to individualize a socially collective situation. This woman's dream does not imply that she should become some sort of Earth Mother who creates an idyllic vegetable garden, or an Amazon who becomes a militant conservationist. It says she needs to find an immediate relation to masculine-oriented collective patterns outside or inside herself and make her influence felt there, as a woman.[10]

A mature social attitude can become, in a woman (or a man) with differentiated feeling, independent of all social issues as such. She may not even be aware of them or of the lessons of history. A particularly good description of this is Virginia Woolf's character, Mrs. Dalloway. This lady was a brilliant London hostess, and another novelist might have shown her in this outward aspect of her life; but Virginia Woolf focuses her attention upon the more subtle quality of her mind and her capacity for social influence through feeling:

She would not say of anyone in the world now that they were this or that. She felt very young; at the same time unspeakably aged. She sliced like a knife through everything; at the same time she was looking on. . . . Not that she thought herself clever, or much out of the ordinary. How she had got through life on the few twigs of knowledge Fraulein Daniels had given them she could not think. She knew nothing; no language; no history; she scarcely read a book now, except memoirs in bed; and yet to her it was absolutely absorbing, all this. . . . Her only gift was knowing people almost by instinct.[11]

Where this kind of feeling is lacking, people may begin to doubt their capacity for adaptation; in looking for an answer to the social ills of their time, as well as for an answer to their own social needs, they are likely to adopt a cynical or despairing attitude or spend their time inventing utopias to keep up hope. Knowing the extreme unwillingness of humanity to follow for very long any one kind of leadership, that search may lead us to recognize, as Sir Herbert Read did in *The Green Child*, that there is a social dilemma which not even the best temporal government can ever fully resolve. Voltaire gave this problem a philosophic answer, urging people to live their lives in accordance with a principle of absolute justice. And here we see why Plato's *Republic*, taking its place as the prototype of all utopian social systems, could never be put into practice, or, if practiced, could not maintain itself for long at any one time; it did not spring from a workable social attitude in which the Eros principle is paramount but is the expression of a philosophic attitude toward government.

People with a well-developed social attitude may be tireless in their efforts to make a humanly workable adjustment which seeks to create unity out of multiplicity, but they know it for what it is: a vision beyond the reality of their immediate place in time, a promise and an incentive—above all, a reminder that this vision has an impressive past.

The aristocratic product of a Colonial first family had a dream while in analysis with me that her family *was* the Church and the State. I therefore knew not to expect, nor did I find, any immediate possibility of cultural change in her; but I did find within the limits of her family's cultural tradition a remarkable capacity to synthesize apparently irreconcilable points of view. She functioned within a cultural tradition which was itself in harmony with many differences of class and creed. What comes to mind is the picture on the title page of Thomas Hobbes's *Leviathan*, (above, page 16), written in the seventeenth century, about the time my patient's ancestors first came from England to America. The enormous figure of a man rises above the hills of a country landscape over which are dotted many villages, hamlets and castles. In the foreground is a large, walled town, with its church prominent in the center. The figure is made up of many, many small people in dress of the period, representing the established human community. We are told that these people embody the "commonwealth"—Hobbes's ideal society, in which people choose their own central authority. But this figure of authority is strictly limited to the three aspects of the society which are recognized as most worthy of respect, symbolized by the crown on his head (kingship), the sword in his right hand (army), and the crozier in his left (clergy).

My patient's psychology illustrated this symbolism very well. Within the framework of her family pattern she rightly considered herself to be humanitarian in the best sense of the word, and she taught me to understand the abiding value of this seventeenth-century image as a modern form of the Anthropos, "societas" embodying the union of "communitas" and "structure" in Victor Turner's sense. This "Leviathan" is a basic image of the society from which we all have emerged and in accordance with which we have functioned until quite recently, as many still try to do. Increasingly and alarmingly, however, today we have no such containing image with which an enlightened government could mediate and control the excesses of religious zeal or militant power.

This is the essence of our discontent with a technocracy, where ecumenical religious groups function autonomously and transitory heads of government control the military forces. Jung never tired of repeating that the State, per se, has become a collective monster[12]— composed of all those people who once were contained in the cultural tradition of their fathers. Actually, the Anthropos has always had its monstrous aspect, and to understand the difference between this dark side and its individually beneficial direction becomes most important, since we no longer tend to see it for what it is.

The Anthropos is not only a Persian Mazdaist and a Gnostic image; it was known in early Christian times as the Son of Man, and this introduces it to us in a form more easily assimilable for our culture.[13] As an archetypal image, however, its magical power can still easily blind us to its actual meaning. This image of Man is just what we find so difficult to see objectively, since it is the image of ourselves in all our confusion—the one and the many, the unified container of all opposites and the multiplicity of all human qualities and potentials which are always flying apart. It is not easy to grasp the real truth stated in the picture of Hobbes's *Leviathan*. At first one sees only the human image, the outline of his body, arms and his very realistic head with its kingly crown, in which form we could say that it represents the power of kingship to control and hold together the opposing forces of worldly (army) and spiritual (clergy) power. But the subtitle of *Leviathan* clearly emphasizes the collective nature of the image: *The Matter, Forme, and Power of A Commonwealth Ecclesiasticall and Civil.*

So it is the authority invested not in one man or group of men but in the people themselves that constitutes the true "body" of the social community. One cannot finally escape the true meaning of this image; it tells us that man is both individual (that is, unified) and collective (that is, a multiplicity), and in his multiplicity he feels himself to be a part of a cultural whole consisting of many parts, which offers the widest view of man's social capacity for feeling.

Because the symbol of the Anthropos is an archetypal image it can of course not be identified with any one cultural attitude, but can act as a unifying focus for all the cultural attitudes. In the case of a religious attitude one finds the answer in some symbolic image of the godhead, in the philosophic attitude some fresh and original idea, or in the aesthetic attitude a great work of art. But since the social instinct and the social attitude are the stuff of human beings themselves, presumably only in their own life-style can they fulfill their social destiny and make their contribution to the social life of their time. Therefore, one must avoid two dangers: that of too much individuality or of too much collectivity.

If one becomes too individualistic, the effect is psychic inflation and isolation from one's fellow men. If one lives too collectively, one becomes uncomfortably deflated and subtly depressed, though one's conformity may bring certain rewards. Individual morality is lowered to the collective norm in which one may find a xenophobic strength. This may become depressing, because its only justification is the soulless expediency of believing that if enough people hold the same beliefs or do the same things, they must all be right. If, however, those values are proposed which embrace both individual and cultural needs, we have the condition necessary for individuation to appear in a social context. Marie-Louise von Franz expresses this as follows:

> In practical terms this means that the existence of human beings will never be satisfactorily explained in terms of isolated instincts or purposive mechanisms such as hunger, power, sex, survival, perpetuation of the species, and so on. That is, man's main purpose is not to eat, drink, etc., but *to be human*. Above and beyond these drives, our inner psychic reality serves to manifest a living mystery that can be expressed only by a symbol, and for its expression the unconscious often chooses the powerful image of the Cosmic Man. [14]

Human here means "cultivated" in the sense of the alchemist Gerhard Dorn's *vir unis* or "true man," of which Jung writes: "The 'true man' expresses the Anthropos in the individual human being. . . . The 'true man' . . . will destroy no valuable cultural form since he is the highest form of culture." [15]

Thus we see that a social attitude arising from conformity to strict ethical principles may in the end provide an avenue to the creation of authentic individuality in a psychological sense.

In addition to the cases I have mentioned of people in whom a social attitude was predominant, I recall a significant example of one in whom the Eros principle was joined with the Logos principle to form such an attitude. This was a woman whose parents held an important position in an academic community. Her father was a professor of philosophy in an old university and she had learned to respect and admire the spirit of inquiry and the daring hypotheses that he and his friends put forth in their pursuit of life's meaning in its broadest sense. But, like Mrs. Dalloway, this woman was primarily interested in people and where she was interested in ideas it was because she was more interested in the person who had them. (One of these she later married.)

Her analysis centered around her need to free herself from the Logos principle as represented by her father and his friends, and what sustained her throughout this period of change was the discovery and development of an effective social attitude. She became a licensed social worker, but this was merely the outward form of the attitude she came to feel had always activated her true interest and sympathy, the quest for social, not intellectual, meaning.

Another woman I treated had a contrasting experience. She had grown up in a family where the social attitude of the parents and their friends colored her education until she left home for college. There she discovered, as a kind of revelation, that although she could recognize the social attitude and value it in others, her own cultural attitude was to become philosophic with a strong support from an aesthetic attitude. In later years this allowed her to become a formidable critic of peoples' motives, but also an appreciative and humorous observer of human behavior. Whereas the social attitude promotes involvement in human affairs or strong empathy with behavioral problems, the philosophic and the aesthetic attitudes achieve detachment or at least a reluctance to produce value judgments that might obscure the true nature of human relations.

If it seems that my examples so far put women in the strongest position as bearers of the social attitude, I hasten to add that we can never overestimate the remarkable achievements that men of our time or of history have made in their individual use of the social attitude. Gandhi is outstanding in this respect, and I think of Martin Luther King and many others who created unifying images to center the maelstrom of political thinking. This does not mean, however, that a social attitude in this sense is always revolutionary or designed to disregard the phenomenon of power politics. Winston Churchill had a social attitude which permitted him to work effectively within the established frame of English society, and in the same period Franklin Roosevelt, from a more liberal social attitude, mobilized public opinion to support him during the years that led up to and included the Second World War. A more truly inspiring figure from this point of view, because we can perceive his resolution of internal conflict both for himself and his country, is Abraham Lincoln during the Civil War.

None of these political world figures, however, can represent the individual nature of the social attitude so well as those who have worked in the field of education where they were called upon to take a liminal position in respect to the prevailing fashion of the times. They have earned their fame by formulating the cultural development of their time in the expression of an individual *Weltanschauung*. I think of Jean Jacques Rousseau as an outstanding example of such a forerunner, as described by Alexander Meiklejohn, who provides an excellent example of this use of the social attitude.[16]

Just as Rousseau outlined the principles of education that were to become necessary as the hierarchical structure of eighteenth-century society changed to become democratic in the nineteenth century, so in our time Meiklejohn outlined the changes in education that would result from effective socialism.

Meiklejohn was the president of Amherst College in the 1920s, until he was asked to resign because his views were considered too socialistic for his time and for this educational institution. He already had perceived the inevitable rise of progressive education in harmony with what was to become reality in the formation of the Welfare State. Accordingly he went on to become one of the leaders of the adult education movement which began in the 1930s. Later he was known for his strong support of the cause of human rights as set down in the Constitution of the United States in many different ways.

My interest in his work from a psychological point of view lies in his insistence that the individual student should not simply be taught to conform to society but to be himself. But in accordance with his social attitude he says:

> We must teach him to "be himself in an organized society." To comprehend the mingling of individual freedom and social authority which that statement intends is the intellectual task of modern education. It is that task to which Rousseau has summoned us.[17]

Meiklejohn, also in this same work, outlines the importance of defining the "cultural themes" which may serve as "bases of plans of teaching." He says,

> If we could do that listening we should have a cultural survey of the society with which we are dealing. ... Cultural history and social psychology have not yet worked out ... such a listing of cultural groupings. ...[18]

He goes on to make suggestions as to the kind of plan that might acknowledge a pattern of culture sufficiently broad to satisfy this educational need and they are informed with common sense and wisdom. Yet they do not do justice to the religious and aesthetic attitudes which I will discuss in the next two chapters.

2

The Religious Attitude

The religious attitude is frequently disguised or distorted by the social attitude, which carries an ethical message and implements it with missionary zeal. This tendency has become especially marked today where a religious attitude, like the aesthetic attitude in the nineteenth century, may seem to be socially irrelevant. Freudian psychology stigmatized the religious attitude as being infantile, and, if appearing in a grown person, regressive. But of course Freud was right to distinguish between infantile religious feelings and later developments as an adult. At the simplest level, religious feeling may be passed on from parents to children unconsciously or may become an experience of religious conversion during childhood or adolescence, but these do not constitute a mature religious attitude. Any child can fall upon its knees in prayer before the ideal image of God derived from mother- or father-images, but these experiences are as transitory as they are fervently wish-fulfilling.

A religious attitude can truly appear only when the rewards and comforts of a parent-child relationship, or dependence upon testimonials of other people's faith, have been outgrown. This takes place normally during adolescence when some significant educational rite of passage ensures separation from emotional dependency upon the family, combined with an awakening consciousness to that principle of Self to which the ego willingly submits.[19] If it were purely a social phenomenon the Self would seem merely to lift the ego into a position of power. T.S. Eliot likens this initial submission of the ego to a superordinate power as "that moment of surrender that a lifetime of prudence can never retract."[20]

True religious emotion depends on an unshakable feeling for its value, not its logic. It is characterized by a childlike simplicity (not infantility) and the immediate conviction that spirit permeates all life. But the affective nature of the religious response is not enough; it requires also some knowledge, some comprehension of the meaning of what has been experienced.

Although the psychologist cannot add anything new to the study of theology and must deny that he is in any formal sense engaged in discovering spiritual facts in his patients' material, he can and must

27

see that his method of research honors the basic principles of theology. I am reminded here of Edward Edinger's claim that the Jungian analyst not only has the right to explore, but even must accept objectively, the metaphysical dimension of life when his patient is struggling with a religious problem.[21] Then, perhaps, he himself may learn something of the personal validity of a religious attitude for the exercise of his specialty. Paul Tillich has made a clear statement in this respect:

> Every theology includes three elements. The first is *theos*, God, or rather God insofar as he makes Himself manifest, the element of revelation. The second is *logos*, rational discourse about what God communicates when he communicates Himself. And the third is *kairos*, the proper moment in time, the time when a theologian must speak to his own age. No systematic theology can dispense with these elements. If the element of *theos*, the element of revelation, is lacking, we are not dealing with theology, though perhaps with the philosophy of religion. If *logos*, the rational word, is lacking, we no longer have theology but ecstasy or nonsense, or both. If the third element, the *kairos*, is lacking, we have merely a dead tradition, and indeed that is often the case with systematic theology.[22]

In adopting this schema for the present study I must first translate it into our psychological language. In this sense *theos* is Jung's Self as god-image perceived and experienced affectively upon its emergence from the world of archetypal images. *Logos* then becomes an intelligible account of this image. *Kairos* is the connection to be made between any individual's spiritual self-confrontation and a similar, general religious problem in contemporary life.

The work we do in analysis diverges very far from theology, of course, and comes closest to religious mysticism in those forms which emphasize the inner experience of a death leading to new life. This is felt to be an initiation of the kind I have mentioned as the experience of late adolescence when either by chance or design, a young person is educated and encouraged to experience the god by himself alone, as different from his larger feeling for the spirit of his peer group. The rite of separation is a kind of purification which gets rid of old attitudes and is followed by an initiatory ordeal of submission to whatever change is destined to occur through evocation of the god-image in any one of its many forms. Actually, these forms are not infinitely varied and can be reduced to a few rather simple themes.

Theos as god-image frequently appears in dreams as one of the four primary elements: air, earth, water or fire, or a combination of them; these in turn are associated with or evolve into a divine animal, plant, child, man, woman or man-and-woman (as divine couple or as hermaphrodite). Examples of this symbolism may be found in any of the great world mythologies but the best known are represented by the Greek gods and goddesses and the stories we have been told of their origins and transformations. We may think of them as men and women, as described by Homer or other poets such as Ovid, but if we study them as described by such modern Greek scholars as Kerényi or Jane Harrison we learn that they have had a whole series of previous incarnations. In one tradition Zeus was a woodpecker, because the woodpecker's behavior told the farmer what weather to expect. Hence Zeus was originally a mantic weather god. Athena, who was supposed to be born fully armed from the head of Zeus, is a late version of the goddess; she was originally a snake or snake charmer as one can see by looking at her tunic which is embroidered with live snakes even in her official portraits. These deities may go back even further; we know, for instance, that Gaia was not originally a woman but the earth itself, that Poseidon was once the water and also earth or bringer of earthquakes, that Hephaestos was fire, that Hermes was a pair of entwined serpents before he became a god and acquired wings. The wings in turn point to an identity with air so that in one of his forms he carries the meaning of one who is intuitively inspired and so he becomes a spirit-guide moving between life and death, between the upper, or conscious, and the lower, or unconscious, worlds.

Putting images such as these together with the archetype of death and renewal, we can find our way among all possible combinations of religious symbolism throughout the cultures of the world. There is, however, a cultural difference in religious attitude between people who start from an original monotheism and those whose religion is primarily polytheistic. The religious experience of death is the same for all, a universal "dark night of the soul," but the renewal which follows it may take two very different roads toward enlightenment: the monotheistic, basically patriarchal, religions favor the image of a resurrection, while polytheism favors the conception of rebirth, with its matriarchal coloring. The first is linear (historically understood) and transcendent which really means "final." The second is recurrent, like the eons or the seasons, and is conceived as cyclic rather than linear—Mircea Eliade's "eternal recurrence of all things."[23]

In contrast to the image of transcendence, the rebirth religions provide us with a significant image of containment. Hence the initiatory rite represented by each of these images is also different. For one, the rite is conceived as "a journey," a mystical approach to the godhead leading to spiritual perfection, a sort of "pilgrim's progress." The other form of transformation, as rebirth, takes place in a sacred precinct, underground chamber or courtyard and the god-image is a symbol of emergence and growth taking place within it like a plant growing in a well-cultivated garden. In alchemy this was symbolized by the Rose Garden. Sometimes these two traditions meet and fuse.

A particularly good example from a patient is a woman's dream in which she was presented with a picture.[24] She said:

> It was an impressive drawing showing the steps of man's aspiration. The drawing resembled an ancient temple or maybe just seven great steps hewn out of stone. The lowermost step represented the mating of man and woman. . . . On the topmost step was "God's image." I was profoundly impressed with this, as if in some way it made man's life meaningful and understandable.

In a rough diagram of steps leading from the union of man and woman to God's image she represented man and woman by their biological symbols; there were seven steps and God's image was a circular blob, by which she designated that which is archetypal and therefore unknown from a purely cultural viewpoint. What is especially striking here is that the drawing is both temple—a symbol of containment, a place where a sacred erotic union takes place—and the stairway to a higher level representing a symbol of transcendence. The two symbols are unified by the number seven which archetypally designates an experience of initiation in the tradition of the mystery religions of antiquity. As I will show in later dream material, the temple points toward rebirth while the stairway points to the symbolism of resurrection, or the attainment of future life after death.

However, a symbol also exemplifies a general religious trend in

William Blake's image of God the Father (from *Book of Job*).

any given historical period, its *kairos*. We find in William Blake's work unmistakable reference to the need for enunciating an individual, human religious need. This seemed to be totally in conflict with the contemporary religions of the time, yet we know now that it reflects a recurrent religious problem of his time to which we can still respond today. On the one hand, Blake was a good Christian and Neo-Platonist; on the other, a sort of religious naturalist, a poet in whom the religious experience was manifested archetypally without cultural antecedents. But there is a third strand of symbolism in his work which is different. It was historically expressed in a stream of alchemical religious philosophy and iconography that followed an underground course from Paracelsus to Jacob Boehme. This tradition maintained a neutral position between the Christian hierarchy of God with the heavenly hosts, and an earthbound religion where the opposites are still together in a state of nature.

In contrast to religion as transcendence or as simple rebirth in nature, today, more certainly than in Blake's time, a new syncretism following an alchemical tradition appears, seeking to realize itself, as in unselfconscious art products, through a symbolism which is reflected in the dream contents of modern, religiously motivated people. This reminds one of that forewarning in Gerhard Dorn's *Musaeum hermeticum*:

> To cause things hidden in the shadow to appear, and to take away the shadow from them, this is permitted to the intelligent philosopher by God through nature. ... All these things happen, and the

eyes of the common man do not see them, but the eyes of the understanding and of the imagination perceive them with true and truest vision.[25]

Aniela Jaffé, quoting this passage, sums up the alchemical tradition as follows:

> The ever repeated attempts to describe the enigmatic qualities and transformations of matter contain such a wealth of religious ideas, so many allusions to a hidden numen, that they endow alchemy with the significance of a *religious movement.*
>   . . . . For the Paracelsists, matter acquired the ineffable quality of an "increatum," and hence was co-existent and co-eternal with God. Since it was conceived as a spiritual and even divine substance, it is hardly surprising that the alchemist's experimental work in the laboratory, his philosophizing, his dream-like immersion in its transformations, and the practical investigation of its qualities took on the character of a religious rite, an *opus divinum.*[26]

The idea of the existence of new life in dead matter requires a totally different religious task from any we have known in our Christian or Judaic traditions. The nearest we can come to it is to remember what the alchemists have said about their experiments of releasing spirit from matter, in "the light of nature." This *lumen naturae* is explained by Jung as follows:

> As the West started to investigate nature, till then completely unknown, the doctrine of the *lumen naturae* began to germinate too. Ecclesiastical doctrine and scholastic philosophy had both proved incapable of shedding any light on the nature of the physical world. The conjecture thereupon arose that just as the mind revealed its nature in the light of divine revelation, so nature herself must possess a "certain luminosity" which could be a source of enlightenment. . . . The more serious alchemists, if we are to believe their statements, were religious people who had no thought of criticizing revealed truth . . . since they endeavoured to prove that the "mystery of faith" was reflected in the world of nature.[27]

What was known as alchemy may then be brought up to date in the modern individual quest for New Being; something as "new" as the scientific discovery of atomic energy, with its conflict between creation and destruction (in accordance with the spirit of *Mercurius duplex*) which points to our present dire need to find some new form of unification by which we may solve the problem of learning how to use nuclear power without its killing us or destroying the world. Jung describes the image of *Mercurius duplex* in saying:

> Here the opposites inherent in the deity are clearly divided. The alchemical parallel to this polarity is the double nature of Mercurius ... and is at the same time their uniting symbol, at once deadly poison, basilisk, scorpion, panacea, and savior.[28]

Philosophical alchemy, then, as a "divine" work, was particularly congenial to men like Jung, whose traditional Christian religious identity has failed them to such an extent that they have to recover from the cultural unconscious a new religious attitude in the *kairos* of our time, which in some ways continues the old tradition of late Greco-Roman nature religions. In that tradition Christ was not so much the sacrificial victim of man's inability to comprehend the life of the spirit; He was the Good Shepherd in the spiritual line of Orpheus. I have elsewhere described Orpheus as the god who remembers Dionysus and anticipates Christ:

> Orpheus was probably a real man, a singer, prophet, and teacher, who was martyred and whose tomb became a shrine. No wonder the early Christian church saw in Orpheus the prototype of Christ. Both religions brought to the late Hellenistic world the promise of a future divine life.[29]

Orpheus differed from Christ in maintaining a connection with the old mystery religions that "brought forth symbols associated with a god-man of androgynous character who was supposed to have an intimate understanding of the animal or plant world."[30]

And so this tradition anticipates what we have described as philosophical alchemy and the doctrine of *lumen naturae*. But it also reflects the transcendent nature of the later Christian mystery which affirms the promise of immortality, as I shall presently describe in detail.

It might be inferred from the ease with which certain analysands can accept the pre-Christian or Oriental religious forms of belief that we analysts take a rather optimistic view of modern man's ability to find a suitable dream or fantasy image of deity, and with only a little adjustment make it comprehensible and then accessible to conscious integration. Such optimism is by no means justified. When the god-image is strongly male and single, i.e., monotheistic, we do not see it as some lovely mythological image. Instead, it may be as horrifying as the Gnostic Abraxas, or Satan, figures which suggest obstruction or persecution, and, if accepted in this guise, may push their victims into a full encounter with the shadow.

To illustrate what we mean by "shadow" in a religious sense, I recall the dream of a woman who entered a church which was filled with a huge dark hostile presence which she thought might be God, but very different from the benevolent fatherly God of her childhood belief. She penetrated further into the church and then saw that this presence became quite simply a rather unappealing, materialistic businessman. She recognized this as the shadow side of her own early idealism, and further discussion allowed her to acknowledge her own legitimate materialism based on the need to support herself financially. This could only come about by revising her whole religious attitude so as to ground it in a new way.

All true redemption resides in our ability to humanize this negative counterpart of the divine image of God. In accordance with this process there may later appear the healing power of the feminine, with its polytheistic coloring, to transform the destructive wrath into a wholesome and love-inspiring unity. This was the experience of Dante, whose journey in *The Divine Comedy* is a religious initiation of this kind.

An initial encounter with the shadow as God's judgment of sinful humanity is shown in the Inferno, followed by a growing awareness of the feminine image (as Beatrice) which brings healing in the Purgatorio and leads to that sense of ultimate union in the Paradiso where the male and female images are suitably balanced. But this can take place only when the personal identity of the individual is strong enough to hold the tension between the warring opposites. Dante had to find his identity between abject humility (shame) on one hand, and the sin of pride (superbia) on the other. Psychologically this is a fundamental pair of opposites experienced by insecure persons in their loneliness as they swing from deflation to inflation; and of the two, the greater danger lies in the tendency to inflation, because it springs from an unrecognized desire for spiritual omnipotence.

Various writers, following Jung's original description of an archetypal pattern known as the *puer aeternus*, have shown how certain young people fall into an attitude of grandiosity which has much in common with Alfred Adler's inferiority complex.[31] It is not inferiority with which such young people identify but with an attitude of superiority which arises as an overcompensation to it;

this is an inflation of ego-consciousness. This attitude often appears (or is intended to appear) as heroic and frequently it is, in the eyes of the world. But the hero-image in this case still clings to its origin in the trickster-figure, he who knows no difference between right and wrong and accepts no discipline other than his own experimental attitude to life. Hence for young people the trickster impulse provides the strongest resistance to initiation, because it seems to be a divinely sanctioned lawlessness that promises to become heroic.[32]

The dream of a patient of mine may further illustrate the relevance of such symbolism. The dreamer was a young man completely at sea about his life in every sense. He had strong vocational aptitudes and a good education but as yet no specific identity or tangible goal. His relationships were ever-changing, as was his place of residence; he was the product of an indulgent family, and his religious beliefs bred a false sense of security. He clearly thought the Lord would always provide. It was difficult to help him, because one did not know how to deliver an appropriate shock to his complacency, how to make him feel exposed to life instead of being artificially protected from it. He did, however, suffer from his situation and had a strong religious feeling that he must, in the Christian sense, lose himself in order to find himself anew.

Then he had a dream which impressed him deeply, making him feel that the problem was somehow taken out of his hands, and that he was being inducted into a primordial religious experience he could not have invented by any flight of his own ideas. He dreamed that he was standing near a table on which lay a huge old book of parchment open before him. As he looked at it a wind blew from the left so strongly that it turned the heavy pages over one by one quite easily. This was no ordinary wind but came from an invisible presence and the whole effect was ghostly. Nearby on his right stood a woman friend and this was reassuring.

To the wind in his dream he associated the breath of the Holy Spirit. The book was philosophic in character, embodying the wisdom he longed to acquire but which in reality he felt he could never seem to remember, no matter how much he read. The woman near him was a recent acquaintance, an older woman, living alone in a style he described as harmonious, peaceful and cultivated. She was a generous hostess and had invited him often to visit her alone or in company with others. There was no erotic physical attraction between them, but she had a strong appeal for him because of her wise comments and her receptiveness to the expression of his ideas. This description of their relationship repeats a familiar pattern found among certain young men who have not yet discovered their true identity and who rely upon the comforting and stimulating influence of a spiritual mother, a *femme inspiratrice*, who can listen and help men discover themselves without making undue emotional demands of her own. There may be genuine erotic interest, but it is secondary to the educational one of helping such a young man create a model for his vocational task.

In the dream this woman is standing on his right, which suggests the side on which he is best adapted to the world. She was cultivated, and from further associations it was clear that the dreamer had much in common with her, owing to the similarity of their social backgrounds. He was the kind of intellectual man who learns at a fairly early age to be at home in the psychic atmosphere of women. Like all *puer aeternus* types, this had its origin in a positive mother identification. Instead of a pure anima-figure represented by some faraway princess or seductive *belle dame sans merci*, or an inviting courtesan, he enjoys certain real women for themselves—women who need not mystify and lure men to love them but can enjoy being simply a companion. In such a relationship there is, of course, some degree of personal projection, but it is of the sort which allows the man to distinguish between the real woman and the anima-image which then becomes, in a manner of speaking, his *inner* feminine companion, she who inspires a love of wisdom rather than a desire for transitory pleasures. One thinks of Diotima in Plato's Socratic dialogues, and we know her specifically religious forms in the Gnostic Sophia or the Shekinah of the Kabbalah, or Tara of Buddhism.

This young man was completely innocent of any such conscious expectation from his new woman friend, and she had no inkling of the fateful role she might be playing in the life of his dream. Both were unprepared for any wind of the Holy Spirit to blow across their relationship. In the dream he is standing before a book which is ancient, unwieldly and whose contents he has difficulty in retaining. Is he to continue to study the book or, instead, cultivate the relationship? Neither, in reality, since each of these alone would lead to a stalemate, to his becoming a bookworm or living too long in a mother-son relationship. Accordingly, the masculine force of the wind blowing the pages of the book implies that learned knowledge is dead compared with the dynamic life of the spirit, and he must now become a man in his own right. Only some such supernatural form of inspiration can, perhaps, breathe new life into those old pages or replace them with wisdom coming from a natural source. But the spirit in this form is too primitive to be enlightening and mainly inspires fear as of some ghostly presence which could destroy him, the book and the friendship as well.

A good many people encounter the spirit only in the form of some spine-chilling apparition, a parapsychological experience usually stimulated by a relationship with someone who has an unconscious mediumistic gift. But this gift is not always unconscious; sometimes it is cultivated by those who may become actual mediums or healers. The possibilities of such bona fide spiritualistic phenomena are of the utmost interest psychologically, just because they appear so unexpectedly and in such improbable types of people. Each time they occur in one of my patients I have to be convinced all over again that such a person is truly mediumistic and not an incurable hysteric.

Frequently hysteria does accompany the true gift and all we see is a person whose trances, visions or voices seem to be attempts to gain power or attract attention. And indeed the power-game may be a special danger, as I.M. Lewis has shown.[33] But we should be careful not to undervalue such a person's talent for prophecy and the poetic understanding of the origins of true religious experience. When these gifts can be accepted, therapy aids the development of a religious attitude as a perfectly legitimate form of cultural identity. Such people learn, and we may learn from them, the art of self-discipline which mediates, as Dante learned to do, between the opposites of inflation and deflation.

The young man whose dream I have related was not himself a mediumistic type of person at all; he was, as the dream suggests, consciously destined to develop to the fullest extent a philosophic attitude. But for this to become real he had first to experience the original religious spirit which animates all true philosophy. Accordingly, he pursued his philosophic interests in his own way, with a new enthusiasm, bringing its contents up to date with the help of subsequent personal analysis. Looking back much later, he felt that this dream was an intrapsychic event which initiated him for the first time into an awareness of what it is to have a religious attitude.

As it brought new life to his intellectual interests it also awakened a new feeling for life itself through the mediation of the woman.

In this man's dream the god-image is represented by air. But the primordial nature of the god-image may be represented in other elemental forms, such as fire, water or earth, as well as air. We have been discussing this elemental form as air, not as such, but air in motion, wind. If we look through any comprehensive work on the history of religions, we find innumerable references to the divine nature of the four elements, and in all cases motion is a constant feature of their appearance. The Holy Spirit can also be fiery or watery. Christ was baptized by water from the Jordan but also by the Holy Ghost and with fire. The rite of baptism was an initiatory experience of renewal intended to cleanse mankind from original sin, which really means bringing about a state of submission necessary to awaken spiritual awareness. Fire, on the other hand, represents the power of the spirit to blaze forth—i.e., to show itself with all its missionary fervor. As Jean Daniélou reminds us:

> It was with the Pentecost that the mission of the church began. As the disciples were gathered in Jerusalem "suddenly there came a sound from heaven as of a rushing, mighty wind, and it filled the house where they were sitting." And there appeared unto them cloven tongues of fire, and it sat upon each of them.[34]

An illustration from the Rabula Codex of A.D. 586 is the earliest surviving representation of the Pentecost.[35] The Virgin Mary stands in the center, with six apostles on each side. Above her the dove of the Holy Ghost descends, and over each head are "the cloven tongues like as of fire" mentioned by the author of Acts. Still close to the source of Christian spirituality, fire and wind denote the unconscious activity which to this day embarrasses the church if it recurs, for how do we know that it will not create the same reformatory zeal for changing the existing church as it did in the first century? In contrast to this symbolism the Virgin stands for that spirit of nonviolence which counteracts the Johanine urge to proselytize,[36] and by her peaceful nature promotes the spirit of submission rather than that of aggression. In contrast to the usual Byzantine differentiation of these elements, expressed anthropomorphically, we should not forget that the original spirit of God was the actual air or water or fire as if they came from the same source.

In Christian mysticism everything streams upward like the

prayers of worshipers, carried aloft on "the wings of the dove."[37] This image comes from Psalms 54:7: "Who will give me wings like a dove and I will fly and be at rest?" On the other side of this coin is the dove descending with its Pentecostal fire to inspire religious action now in this world. Yet from their place of origin in the archetype of the Spirit they are one and the same thing.

I need hardly point out what is so glaringly absent in these elemental Christian forms of Spirit: that element which the ancients called earth. Earth, with or without vegetation, appears commonly in modern dreams just as it so often appeared in alchemy as the *coagulatio* or transformation of matter. This was omitted in Christianity, as well as in Judaism, because it was thought that everything "earthy" was alien to the heavenly spirit. By contrast, another form of spirit was thought to find release through its own activity, its own process of fermentation and growth, as in Paracelsus' "light of nature." No matter how enlightened or uplifted we may be by our religion, modern people seem to suffer from a deep sense of alienation from that Earth to which our ancestors traced their origin and from which they derived their main security by placing it cosmologically in the very center of their universe.

A man once came to me to ask what I thought was the meaning of an impressive dream he had had following the death of his father. The death of a man's father is of great importance psychologically and is usually felt to be so by most men. In light of their dreams it appears to be closely related to their religious development. The man whose father has died before he (the son) is ready for it is in danger of being thrown into a crucial period of self-doubt because he is called upon psychologically to shoulder the responsibility for his life and his family before he is fully prepared. If on the other hand he is ready for this event he may feel the invigorating sense of a new coming-of-age, with a determination to complete his own mature cultural task.

The man who brought me his dream was mature in this sense, as he had been for a long time free of his father's influence and was ready for his father's death—a little too free, in that he wished he could have had greater love and respect for his father, especially in his adolescent years. He had looked instead to other men's fathers to learn how to conduct himself. It was difficult to see why this was so, since his father had actually had a highly successful career as a mining engineer and was universally loved by his associates and friends.

But the son felt there was something missing, which he could only describe as a lack of some form of cultural consciousness. He said, "My father didn't really know what cultural life is all about. Whenever we went to theaters or concerts or museums or churches he had no opinion of his own and apparently no real experience in relation to them. In the end he had no religious interests to comfort him in his old age, although my mother was a naturally religious woman of considerable intellectual capacity. He sometimes worried about his physical weaknesses and in his old age allowed himself to be read to by a Christian Science practitioner, but never expressed any wish to regard this as a satisfactory religion. Ethically he was perfectly sound, and his morality echoed the praiseworthy sentiments of a Christian's love for his neighbor; but I wondered why he never expressed any original religious feeling of his own."

With this background the man told me his dream:

> My father is not present in the dream, but it takes place in one of those caves he must have explored many times in the search for precious metals to be mined. The cave in my dream reminds me of one of the abandoned tunnels in the vicinity of Virginia City, where my father once took me. At that time he told me fascinating stories about the Comstock Lode and the men who mined it, many of whom he had known in his youth.
>
> While walking in this tunnel-like cave I came upon a huge oval object covered with the greyish-yellow earth in which it had been embedded for centuries. It was a dinosaur's egg. I was very impressed, and instead of thinking of it as a fossil I wondered if it still contained the living embryo which might grow, causing the creature inside to break out after all these centuries.

The dream had impressed this man because the dinosaur's egg gave him a feeling that it had to do with his father's unrealized potential for attaining some kind of cultural consciousness, especially of a religious kind. But why, he wondered, did it take this most unlikely, grotesque form?

Further discussion of this man's family revealed some interesting facts which led me to believe that his father had never developed any cultural attitude of his own, especially not a religious attitude, because his own father and the other members of the family on both sides were too busy making the physical adjustments necessary for settling a pioneering community in the Far West. Cultural matters did not concern them and were handed over to those women who cared to occupy themselves with such things. Life presented these men with immediate tangible, practical or political problems from dawn to dusk, from one year's beginning to another. They loved the challenge and rose to it magnificently. Technological progress was all that really interested them, and its many exciting possibilities for development kept them fully occupied. The simple joys or sorrows of family life provided all the cultural life they seemed to need.

It seemed to me that the dream was telling the son of a part of the story he did not know: that the men of his father's generation had paid a specific price for failing to contribute to the cultural life of their families; they had neglected the basic religious principle of rebirth which allows spiritual as well as biological life to flourish. When such an important cultural task is ignored, it does not merely stand still, waiting for its next development to be furthered. It regresses, taking on an archaic form. In the dream this form is not even humanly conceived. It is like the fossil embryo of a saurian creature belonging to a prehistoric age. Something as old and as earth-bound as this was needed as a symbol to show this man how far down he might have to dig to recover that religious principle that had remained unborn in his immediate ancestral line. Could this image be born again into life in spite of the absence of the right conditions for germination, or was it to be regarded as dead forever, a mere fossil?

I put these alternative interpretations before the man and he considered them for a long time before he expressed his own reaction. At length he said he had a sad feeling about the egg. He hated to acknowledge the truth that his father, and perhaps himself, too, as his father's son, had to go through life without some vital experience of rebirth or renewal. On the other hand, he felt he had experienced genuine psychological changes and that he could, now that his father was dead, develop further in this sense. What surprised him, but now made him hopeful, was the reference to a form of renewal that was completely unspiritual in the conventional sense. He finds it in the earth—that same earth where his father had taken him when still full of pride in his worldly (i.e., earthly) career. Only by taking another look at this technological pattern could he perhaps see now what was positive in it, that he was not to look for spiritual insight or guidance only from above but to consider that it might emerge from below, from an unexpectedly ancient source of life, and so inadvertently his father may have done him a special service. This insight helped to correct the one-sidedness of his own intellectual attitude, with its unquestioned assumption that all spiritual experience is heaven-sent, and what comes from below is nothing but common clay.

This man's dream image reminded him to include the earthly dimension of religious feeling that could, in the sense of Teilhard de Chardin's religious philosophy, reconcile the findings of modern science with traditional Christian belief. Why should the Holy Spirit not be immanent in the scientific certainties arrived at through the work of Galileo, Newton, Darwin or Einstein, just as truly as in the ancient cosmogonies which were also created by the best minds of their time?[38]

Actually there is every reason to think that we are entering a period in which Christianity must ground itself anew in some such revision of theology in accordance with biological and physical principles. But we must not, on scientific evidence alone, gloss over the very real conflict this must create in the people whose religious orientation is still bound to the doctrine that the soul is imprisoned in this life, in this body, and longs to return to its heavenly home. Christianity is still unconsciously, if not consciously, based on the Fall of Man, and its main function is to teach people how to rise again, how to transcend this mortal state. This tradition contains an inborn hope for many people of the miraculous possibility of attaining some kind of immortality, and it has been strengthened throughout Christian history by large transfusions of Neo-Platonism derived from the earlier Orphic tradition which resulted in the Christian doctrine of the body as a prison.[39]

Behind this whole tradition there is the strong supporting structure of monotheism, which in early tribal societies may have been created out of the original spirit of shamanism. Where this tradition appears in higher cultures we find that renewal is thought to be the achievement of a final state of spiritual serenity, now or in the world beyond. In the mainline Christian tradition we find a striving toward the realization of final things, to be determined by a Last Judgment. Buddhism postulates a transcendent spiritual state which expects to leave all things behind, whether temporal or final, and to attain freedom from all imaginable human needs. In contrast to this the Christian religion affirms the reality of this world as a basis for learning about the next, and it maintains a lively egoistic ambition to attain the blessed state. It proclaims: "I know that my redeemer liveth and . . . in my flesh I shall see God." (Job 19:25)

Both of these attitudes, different as they are, remind one of shamanistic ecstasy, the Buddhist representing the shaman's "magic flight" and the Christian denial of any real barrier between life and death for the faithful. For each, the assumption of some kind of spirit-world is implicit, but this too is transmuted into the quest for the essential Buddha-nature or the achievement of an Imitatio Christi. The Byzantine mystic, like the Buddhist yogi, anticipates ultimate liberation, but in that tradition it evokes a much more subtle form of the "magic flight," as we saw, "on the wings of the dove." Daniélou's further elaboration of this image therefore becomes historically meaningful:

> Thus the Platonic theme of the "wings" and the Gospel theme of the "dove" are brought together by way of the Psalmist's "wings of the dove" . . . the connection between "the wings of the soul" and the dove of the Jordan carries us back to Gnosticism. Hippolytus, describing the system of Basilides, writes: "The (second) sonhood wings itself with some such wing as that wherewith Plato, Aristotle's teacher, equips the soul in the *Phaedrus*, and Basilides calls the same not a wing but (the) Holy Spirit."[40]

The precious piece of Greco-Hebraic syncretism which this passage reveals was kept well hidden from mainline Christianity when it was not suppressed altogether as heresy by the early Christian Fathers. As I.M. Lewis points out, the ecstatic aspects of mainline religion were moralized, thus losing their mystical religious character.[41] Then the shaman became a priest, and imperceptibly the priest became a political director of conscience or even a social dictator.

This progression of events has been illustrated in the development of Christianity by political dissension beginning with Luther's Proclamation and continuing until the end of the seventeenth century. Then there briefly reappeared a philosophic revival of the archetype of transcendence in the eighteenth century, when the medieval social structure itself was about to collapse. This consisted of a revival of interest in Plato and Neo-Platonism which colored much of the poetry and literature of the Romantic period following the French Revolution. In summing up the characteristics of this whole tradition we may single out the ascetic tendency to prefer spirit to matter and to improve the conditions of this earth only so that the soul at death may leave the body and wing its way heavenward, with the least effort or delay. The wings, in one tradition, are the virtues we acquire in this life through self-restraint, patience, compassion, self-sacrifice and selfless devotion to higher things, recognized as doing the will of God. This omits the wholesome reshaping of an earth-oriented religion of rebirth, which thus, by way of compensation, makes its reappearance in the unconscious of modern people with a new urgency.

And so the cycle of religious beliefs comes full circle, as it always has and presumably always will. Only human beings, through acceptance and mediation of their paradoxical nature, may unify them in an individual way, temporarily, in the light of their spiritual revelation from above or, at certain times, in the light of nature from below. Thus religion, in spite of its origin in ecclesiastic ritual or the practice of magic, may become a vehicle for individual development, promoting not religion as dogma but a true religious attitude, in harmony with the psychology of individuation.

3

The Aesthetic Attitude

Unlike the social attitude or the religious attitude, the aesthetic attitude exists without any sense of duty whatsoever, and in the sphere of human relations it is content with naming human qualities or attributes without any attempt to pass judgment or win approval. These observations have the character of being part of a "just-so" story without any real moral. The aesthetic attitude is also independent of philosophic or religious attitudes, as is proclaimed in the closing lines of Keats's "Ode on a Grecian Urn:" " 9'Beauty is truth, truth beauty'—that is all/ Ye know on earth, and all ye need to know";[42] and the preceding lines inform us that the secret of this "beauty" lies in its timelessness, creating a vivid impression of immortality.

Schiller's aesthetic attitude, as described by Jung, also stresses the unity of beauty and truth.[43] The artist's creation of the beautiful object, or the experience of those who respond to it, depends upon a kind of apperception which could be considered a delusion if there were not an aesthetic attitude to accord it cultural validity. Again Keats's ode may be cited as an example. The Grecian urn is an object we have not seen nor ever will see as Keats saw it; but we accept it as real insofar as we accept Keats's poem about it as a work of art:

> ... O Attic shape! Fair attitude! with brede
> Of marble men and maidens overwrought,
> with forest branches and the trodden weed;
> Thou, silent form, dost tease us out of thought
> As doth eternity ...[44]

The reader's response to the poem, as well as Keats's apperception of the object which inspired it, affirms its special kind of "truth" as being "just-so," needing no argument to justify its existence.

We must emphasize that this attitude is the most reliable form of cultural orientation not only for poets, artists or their special public, but for many quite ordinary people as well. However, anyone in a mature stage of development may encounter a special problem in the age from which we are now emerging, which had abandoned the traditional forms by which the aesthetic attitude was honored and included as a part of cultural life as a whole. In the Christian Middle Ages and on into the Renaissance, artists were members of a congregation of believers in a more or less common faith expressed in Christian architecture, iconography and music. Kenneth Clark's film series and book, *Civilisation*, beautifully demonstrates the variety and social relevance of the aesthetic attitude in Christian history. Romanticism and, later, the Victorian age with its utilitarian ethic so effectively triumphed over earlier aesthetic traditions that anyone who fully espoused an aesthetic attitude tended to withdraw to the narrow confines of a cultish movement known as Art for Art's Sake. During that same century, however, a few brave prophets proclaimed the right of an aesthetic attitude to travel again in the mainstream of cultural life—notably, Schopenhauer and Nietzsche. Thomas Mann writes:

> Nietzsche inherited from Schopenhauer the proposition that "life as representation alone, seen pure or reproduced in art, is a significant spectacle—the proposition, that is, that life can be justified only as an aesthetic phenomenon."[45]

From the vantage point of modern psychology we can see that Nietzsche's aestheticism contained the seeds of its own destruction, just as the movement of Art for Art's Sake did. It found itself in an isolated position and, insofar as its followers sought to escape the social reality of their times, it tended more and more to isolate them even from each other. Hence, at the beginning of the twentieth century, psychoanalysis quite logically anathematized aestheticism as a form of misplaced autoeroticism. Even Jung, though from a much more valid psychological standpoint, at first accepted the Lipps-Worringer hypothesis that aestheticism is a form of self-divestiture.[46] His use of the term "aesthetic" frequently has a pejorative sense, which suggests that all creativity is based on some kind of psychic dissociation.

Times have changed since then, and we know that aesthetic sensibility, as such, is not in itself good or bad, healthy or ill. It may be a drawback or a boon, a dreary limitation or a glowing advantage for its possessor, and no one believes any longer that art or the aesthetic attitude can be defined only as preciosity. At its best it opens its devotees not only to art but to the same creative exuberance in expressing an affirmative feeling for life that the painters or architects or musicians of the great periods enjoyed when aesthetic appreciation was still a fully recognized part of the whole culture. But an expression of faith in an aesthetic attitude is not enough. So let us once again carry this aspect into its appropriate depth. We then may be able to demonstrate its rightful place in the whole spectrum of culture.

In a former paper, I sought to show that artists know themselves best through the aesthetic attitude, and this is why they tend to maintain that creativity comes not only from the unconscious, as so many practitioners of depth psychology have claimed, but is also the result of conscious deliberation and choice.[47] The work of art is not a spontaneous product of the unconscious even in those works where the presence of some archetypal content is obviously present. Every artist feels that his work is conceived in a union of inspiration with the artist's specific craft. For example, we have long known that personal memories or reflections are not literary works of art unless writers can translate them into an impersonal story form, with all that this implies in the artistic choice of things remembered. If Proust in *Remembrance of Things Past* had simply presented the factual memories of his childhood they would merely provide an embarrassing exposure of obsessional mother-bound narcissism. His perfected work redeems his neurotic retirement from the world at a comparatively early age, because instead of the musings of a chronic asthmatic, he brought forth from his cork-lined room the pure gold of art.

Even when the writer leaves his own personal life history behind, this is still the case. Plunging into the deep unconscious, as Joyce did in *Finnegan's Wake*, we might assume that he then abandoned normal culture-consciousness for the shifting chaos of undisciplined emotional forces. But this was not so. Joyce balanced his awareness of the deep unconscious with a conscious purpose, which he had already clearly stated in *The Portrait of the Artist as a Young Man*. His autobiographical hero, Stephen Daedalus (a name combining a Christian saint, St. Stephen, with the legendary Greek artificer and inventor, Daedalus), is first of all a youth identified with a religious attitude until, awakening to a sense of himself as an artist, he comes into possession of an aesthetic attitude as the cultural compass for his life's journey. Instead of leading him into self-divesture, alienation from life or escapism, this new attitude rescues him from bondage to his parents. In his diary

Stephen announces his decision to become a conscious literary artist and craftsman:

> Welcome O Life! I go to encounter the reality of experience and to forge in the smithy of my soul the uncreated conscience of my race. ... Old Father, old artificer, stand by me now and forever in good stead.[48]

Joyce took a road which, though seemingly a labyrinth, can clearly be recognized today as having a distinct design and, as Joseph Campbell and Henry Robinson so clearly show,[49] his creative destiny was similar to that of other revolutionary writers of his generation such as T. S. Eliot and Thomas Mann. The first task of that generation lay in a destruction of the decadent art forms of nineteenth-century middle-class culture, with an exposure of the unconscious, "repressed" elements of the personality we know so well from psychoanalytic theory and which Jung has called the personal unconscious. These writers showed that this aspect of the unconscious was repressed as much from middle-class propriety as from some merely personal problem. Joyce traversed this state in *Ulysses*, and the aesthetic attitude expressed in *The Portrait of the Artist* was changed, becoming less and less personally conditioned as it moved finally to a deeper layer of culture in *Finnegan's Wake*. This leads to an invocation of Ireland's Celtic history embodied in the ancient hero-figure, Finn McCool, and suggests a death and rebirth pattern (based on a pun, Finn Again) emerging from an archetypal, not a personal or known, cultural-historical level, and we realize that Joyce, the artist (Stephen Daedalus), is fully engaged in forging "the uncreated conscience" of his race.

Without going further into the world of literary criticism where so many differing viewpoints contend with one another, I think these examples, brief as they are, show one thing clearly: that an aesthetic attitude appropriate for a given tradition in a given period is universally experienced by all who are alive to this aspect of the culture-pattern. Though it may be differently conceived and differently expressed—and certainly also differently received—the aesthetic task of any one artist in any one time is felt to depend less upon his inspiration than upon his conscious will. His true vocation, like that of Joyce, announces itself in advance; the goal may or may not be attained, but its intent is implicit from beginning to end.

An aesthetic attitude of the period corresponding to the work of

Joyce or Eliot or Mann has a particular relevance for the period which preceded it, as well as for our own period which followed. The new art of this century sought to destroy not only the outworn social or religious attitudes of the nineteenth century but the aestheticism as well. In the Art for Art's Sake movement it had severed its relation with other cultural attitudes and had self-consciously tried to stand alone. The effect of repudiating this attitude was to ensure that an aesthetic attitude appropriate to our own time would not stand alone, but would be reconnected with other aspects of culture and might therefore become freshly enlivening. In the visual arts, the painting of Paul Klee with its exposure of strange symbolic forms and the painting of Kandinsky are examples of this change. It paved the way for the best of surrealism and the non-objective school of artists that followed.

In observing people, many of them my patients, who responded enthusiastically to the book and film series, *Civilisation*, I noticed that they all had a strongly developed aesthetic attitude; thus they responded naturally to Clark's expression of his own personal aesthetic attitude, which allowed him to demonstrate the significant changes in Western cultural history since the early Middle Ages through the art, architecture and music of the various periods. The response of these people was positive not because he demonstrated works of art, most of which they already knew fairly well, but because he showed in countless subtle ways how the aesthetic expression of each period could be used to explain more clearly the nature of social, religious and philosophical change. In this film we find a living example of those modern men who are no longer content to look at art in museums segregated from other aspects of culture, but who mean to relate it to the whole culture as art had been in the past, before the decadence of Victorian taste elevated social and scientific attitudes beyond all others.

I also noticed that Lord Clark's film series irritated those art historians who wish to keep the field of their study single and pure, and that people in whom the social, religious or philosophic attitudes are strongest found a great deal to complain of. The ethical consistency of a social attitude, the logic of a philosophic attitude or the transcendent nature of a religious attitude are evidently unsatisfied by the sensuous irrationality of the aesthetic attitude. Yet it is frequently just what these other attitudes need to keep them from petrifaction.

In the *I Ching* we find an interesting example of an aesthetic attitude. Hexagram 22, *Pi*, is translated as *Grace*:

> This hexagram shows a fire that breaks out of the secret depths of the earth, and blazing up, illuminates and beautifies the mountain, the heavenly heights. Grace—beauty of form—is necessary in any union if it is to be well ordered and pleasing rather than disordered and chaotic.[50]

We are told that "this is the world of art" which brings "the tranquility of pure contemplation," but sooner or later all beauty of form "will appear to have been only a brief moment of exaltation. . . . For this reason Confucius felt very uncomfortable when once, on consulting the oracle, he obtained the hexagram of Grace."[51] Jung, in his commentary on the *I Ching*, observes that this reaction by Confucius "is reminiscent of the advice given to Socrates by his daemon—'You ought to make more music'—whereupon Socrates took to playing the flute."[52] If, as I think, Confucius may be regarded as a man in whom the social attitude to culture was predominant, and Socrates was clearly an outstanding representative of the philosophic attitude, we can understand their tendency to neglect the aesthetic attitude and to have to be reminded—in Confucius' case, uncomfortably—to include it.

This passage in the *I Ching* illustrates the most important quality of any basic response to pure beauty, its evanescence, which Shelley likened to "a fading coal."[53] Perhaps this helps to account for the sense of unreliability it conveys compared with other forms of cultural experience—especially the religious experience with its view of what eternally exists behind the visible universe, even if now we see it only "through a glass darkly." Compared with this or with the determination of the social order, the aesthetic attitude may therefore seem wayward. But while this may be true for what Joseph Campbell calls the moment of "aesthetic arrest,"[54] the aesthetic attitude, in the sense I use it here, is made of firmer stuff. In my discussion of the four attitudes (chapter five) I shall point out its affinity with a devotion to science which we know is one of the most sustaining aspects of any culture in maintaining a high degree of patient observation of the phenomena of nature, promoting mankind's consciousness of its place in the world. Natural science is essentially dependent upon that type of observation by which the pure aesthetic experience is stabilized in an attitude from which fresh discoveries can be made.

In the practice of Jungian analysis, many analysands are people with a highly developed aesthetic sense which has distinguished them, but which may also have helped to isolate them, an example of what Marion Woodman has so well described in *Addiction to Perfection: The Still Unravished Bride*. They come to analysis seeking, among other things, to be released from this isolation, although they frequently think they are coming to obtain a psychological sanction for maintaining their aesthetic attitude. Therefore, they become at first even more strongly defended against relinquishing their isolation than they were before.

I have come to recognize that this can be a strong form of initial resistance to analysis. A young instructor of English at a university came to me for treatment and had to overcome his initial doubt that he could trust me, because he felt he knew more about literature than I did. A poet told me she could not go even to Jung for analysis, much as she would like to, because Jung would not understand the subtleties of the English language. One patient dreamed that she could see only the natural world through a glass window which was pointed like the prow of a ship. Outside she could see the water of the bay and the islands beyond, but this ship's prow was going nowhere. In all these cases I noticed a real stasis of feeling—feeling for life. Instead there was a sense of isolation which comes from looking at life, rather than from experiencing its vital force. They were highly self-conscious and able to objectify their lives and relationships to a remarkable degree, but there was a sense that nothing new was happening to them. They longed for an experience that would change them, but whenever such an opportunity came their way they tried to organize it so as once more to aestheticize it. Such people are like actors in a play, or like painters composing a picture, and so they really suffer from living, as it were, behind a glass wall.

In overcoming this initial resistance, it is interesting to see how they adapt to further treatment and what happens to their aestheticism. It might be supposed that if one succeeded in smashing the glass wall of their isolation they would be happily accessible to a new humanism or to nature, in response to which they might free their true instinctual energies for life. On the contrary, at first they merely turn their aesthetic perceptions toward the new objects; if toward a person they establish a transference which has many features of the old walled-off aestheticism; and if toward nature, they establish an equally aesthetic transference to that. True enough, they may come considerably closer to life than they were, because any transference immediately mobilizes a desire for union with the object so that there is a heightened expectation of new things to come. But this may still be far removed from reality. If the transference falls upon a person, this person is considered as perfect as a work of art, and even his or her manifest weaknesses may seem to embellish the whole picture. If the transference is made to nature, this too may create the image of some kind of perfection. Nature, in the Romantic era, was sublime; what had been despised during the previous centuries as frightening, uncouth, dirty, only enjoyed when properly cultivated in some carefully laid out garden or park, became suddenly a beautiful, ennobling spectacle.

It is true that these Romanticists may not always maintain Apollonian serenity, but may wish to fling themselves into nature's arms. Instead of contemplating a mountain view, they shoot the rapids of her liveliest streams. In this case, says Jung, quoting Nietzsche, "Man is no longer the artist, he has become the work of art."[55] This allows the dangerous, even the ugly facts of nature to be accepted as part of the total aesthetic experience; here the Apollonian goes over into its opposite, the Dionysian. The Apollonian principle maintains its contemplative detachment, whereas the Dionysian principle provokes an impulse to live out, dance out or actively represent an at-oneness with the object as person, animal, plant or stone. In this case, working in clay or sculpting may become a powerful activity. For people who have not had a sufficient range of aesthetic appreciation or expression, a shift to the opposite of their accustomed mode of functioning may be very enlivening and therefore temporarily therapeutic. An intro-verted aestheticism of the pictorial or literary kind may then go over into its opposite, or an exaggerated tendency to live out every impulse may be channeled into poetry, listening to music or pursuing the observations of natural science. These alternative patterns may interact in all sorts of meaningful ways.

At a certain point the opposites may seem to be reconciled by means of the aesthetic attitude itself. Jung has commented on this in a criticism of Nietzsche's standpoint toward the Greek tradition:

> Nietzsche, like Schiller, had a pronounced tendency to credit art with a mediating and redeeming role. The problem then remains stuck in aesthetics—the ugly is also "beautiful," even beastliness and

evil shine forth enticingly in the false glamour of aesthetic beauty. The artistic nature in both Schiller and Nietzsche claims a redemptive significance for itself and its specific capacity for creation and expression.[56]

Jung saw that "in the struggle between Apollo and Dionysus and in their ultimate reconciliation the problem for the Greeks was never an aesthetic one, but was essentially religious."[57] Later on Jung shows how in poetry and in art in general a symbol seems to be created, which has the function of uniting the opposites. So he seems to relent, reaccepting the aesthetic solution, up to a point, as a solution of the problem. "We cannot . . . afford to be indifferent to the poets," writes Jung, "since in their principal works and deepest inspirations they create from the very depths of the collective unconscious," so they "have an educative influence on their own and succeeding generations."[58] But the deeper the process of creating a symbol, the greater the danger of its contamination with other symbols—many of an archaic nature. Hence, says Jung, "an imperfectly understood yet deeply significant content usually has something morbid about it."[59]

This is the point at which a psychological interpretation may become necessary. We saw how the unifying symbol may arise from a social attitude—the Anthropos in his social aspect—and how symbols may be created out of the religious attitude, but we should not limit our view of the symbol to any one cultural expression. Thus, even Jung falls into a cultural prejudice when he implies that the symbol is basically only religious. At the point where the symbol emerges from the collective unconscious I think it may take any one of the four cultural forms I have defined.

The aesthetic attitude, unlike the others, *values the symbol for itself alone,* and is untroubled by its contradictory or ambiguous qualities. Accordingly, I have found that some aesthetic appreciation then is absolutely essential in mediating certain conflicts. In an analysis we may first try to bridge them by eliciting free associations concerning the imagery of the conflict, a straightforward procedure in the old Freudian sense, where one expects to get the first thing which pops into the patient's mind concerning a dream or fantasy, or even involuntary emotional reactions. But this tends to remain on a superficial level unless some other type of associative activity is brought into being. Here is our function of apperception or *way of combining two or more apparently incompatible things at the same moment without any disturbance to the rational mind.* It must seem as natural as humor, where incompatible elements are blended in a surprising but perfectly comprehensible way.

I recall a patient where the essential psychological meaning of an approach to art, together with creation of spontaneous art forms, was especially significant. I shall first quote from a previous paper:[60]

> This woman was already in the process of individuation when she started her analysis two years previously. At that time she had a well-developed aesthetic attitude and had even done some original creative work in painting and gardening. But her attitude had been perfectionistic and had cut her off from certain aspects of life, which illustrates what Jung originally stated about art for art's sake leading to abstraction or self-divestiture. But the material she brought me did not indicate that she should abandon her aesthetic attitude. In the course of her analysis, however, it underwent a significant change. The tendency to aestheticize life changed into a capacity to receive the meaning of life into whatever aesthetic framework she could devise, and this was made possible by a very active period in which she took great pains to learn to interpret her own dreams. In this she was unusually successful, though she needed my comments and corrections as she went along.
>
> The dream which expressed this activity is as follows:
> "I am making something like calligraphy on scrolls or clay tablets. It is something which starts very small and then when I put it in water it expands to full size. The art is to know how long to leave it in the water. It is very tricky. Then I put the scrolls or tablets in the sun to dry. I don't know where these things have come from, whether I have made them or only developed them, but they are considered my works of art. I want to take them home with me, which I cannot do alone without being helped by a friendly man who carries my heavy suitcase and buys my bus ticket for me."

Her explanation of the dream continues:

> "Is this man an animus-figure? I am glad he did not continue with me to my home. I got what I wanted from him, the lifting of the heavy load, and he bought me a ticket to my next destination and saw me on my way. The calligraphy represents the content of my dreams to be deciphered. First they are formed in miniature and then, through 'soaking in water,' they are enlarged and then dried in the sun. They become full creative works of art with a written message in beautiful writing."

Interpreting this dream, I described the works of art as the dream content, the "soaking in water" till it is enlarged as the amplification, and the drying in the sun as the period of rendering the specific inner meaning accessible to consciousness. So far, the meaning of the dream seemed quite clear, and accordingly I felt free to ask my patient if she would allow me to use her dream for my paper about the artist's relation to the unconscious, which she willingly did.

As is so often the case, further reactions and other dreams threw some doubt upon the validity of this interpretation. Upon reading my paper, the woman said she was embarrassed by the use I had made of her dream because she felt it wasn't yet true that she had developed the scrolls. She had been guilty of identifying reality with her intuition, a common failing of people in whom this function is highly developed. They seem to care for "the reality of the possibility"[61] more than about reality itself. I, as a Jungian analyst with intuition as my superior function, had easily fallen in with this because of its prospective viewpoint, and so she and I had both undervalued the function of sensation needed to pin down and really apply our intuitions to this woman's actual life.

This came out in her association of the name Nick Gracianos to the animus-figure in her dream. She said:

> What I had not bothered to track down at that time was the name, Nick Gracianos, who turns out to be a big-time gambler rum-runner of the thirties. So the helpful man whom I associate with the friendly creative animus is also a dangerous trickster. This brought home to me my tricky, shallow use of the aesthetic attitude. I had played all my life with my natural ability for the aesthetic . . . I did not go down within to search for a deeper meaning in the unconscious, the true message on the scrolls.
>
> Anyway I was determined to drop my interest in art until it welled up unbidden; I purposely blinded myself to any flower arrangement or garden aesthetic. No longer did I look at paintings with an eye for balance, color or composition. I refused to judge myself or others in like manner.
>
> Then one day I scribbled sumi ink on paper as a child would do—bound I would pay no attention to past-learned, calligraphic techniques. I see now I was searching for a way to redeem my doubts of my aesthetic attitude, sending them down deep to wait for the genuine "faint scratchings" from within to announce their return in their own time.

Out of this whole process of introversion she brought forth a totally unexpected insight and represented it in a piece of sculpture. Although this had the genuine character of an art work, it was primarily relevant to herself alone, and I would not even try to describe it here for fear of exposing it and her to a critique of its artistic merit. In any case, this is not indicated since it opened her to a new phase of her experience of self-discovery, involving not only one but the other cultural attitudes as well. It transformed the aesthetic attitude itself into that form of awareness which lies on the other side of all specific cultural values per se, or rather that which returns it to the matrix from which all cultural values originally spring.

In the humble products of art which are created during the course of a Jungian analysis, such as my patient here produced, we can affirm the authenticity of this viewpoint where the aesthetic attitude reaches its greatest moments of fruition, but these psychologically motivated amateur artists would themselves maintain that, at the point of their greatest insight, they have passed beyond art and have entered a new phase of life.

There may, of course, remain a valid doubt about the possibility of separating art from religion, since in their original manifestations they so often seem to be identical—the religious cult object of worship, the icon, being also a work of art. However true this may be on an archaic level, it is not true for modern culture as we know it. Goethe, with one of his characteristically brilliant perceptions, states that art and religion are culturally different, and indirectly shows why the archetypal image is the only real criterion for either:

> Religion ... stands in the same relation to art as any other vital material. Faith and want of faith are not the organs with which a work of art is to be apprehended. On the contrary, human powers and capacities of a totally different character are required. Art must address itself to those organs with which we apprehend it; otherwise it misses its effect. A religious material may be a good subject for art but only insofar as it possesses general human interest. The Virgin with the Child is on this account an excellent subject, and one that may be treated a hundred times, and always seen again with pleasure.[62]

Goethe's example of an archetypal image is a singularly appropriate choice from the point of view of modern depth psychology since it evokes the memory of the state of being at one with the mother as primordial source of all life, one which in turn is

Mother and Child, sculpture by Henry Moore.

suggestive of the original emergence of individuality from the depths of all dream-like imaginings. The Divine Child embodies the whole mythologem of this emergence of the Self wherever we find it, and it is convincing just because all of us are drawn to return in memory to that original state from which our conscious identity first emerged. The artistic representation of the image then renders it accessible to consciousness because of its own self-contained value. That is why some degree of artistic creativity along with our capacity to respond to it is felt to be necessary, and why the mere repetition of an outdated form of the image fails to satisfy us. For instance, Renaissance paintings of the Virgin or Virgin and Child may no longer evoke the response which a modern sculpture, say by Henry Moore, accomplishes, because the latter expresses the archetypal image in the spirit of our time, a time which requires that the image of a heavenly Madonna may again be seen in her chthonic aspect as an ancient Earth Mother existing in art before heaven was created.

Actually the Christian version of Mother and Divine Child has always had a tendency to desert heaven for an earth-connected religious feeling. The Byzantine icons of Madonna with the infant Christ which influenced Cimabue and Giotto are monolithic earth-mothers, and a cathedral which possesses a Black Virgin is especially holy because of her appeal for the simplest of people, peasants, whose religion has not really changed much with the coming of Christianity and who continue to worship in the spirit of the old Tellus Mater, who was the actual earth before she became personified.

In our description of the aesthetic attitude we have tried to follow one similar to our treatment of the social attitude. No one attitude is quite like any other, yet they all seem to obey the same developmental law. Arising from an archetypal matrix, they then come to belong to a cultural complex or culture pattern, which helps to define the cultural differences between them.

4

The Philosophic Attitude

When I meet the philosophical attitude, either in patients or in friends, I am impressed by their scrupulosity in getting to the truth of things. Such people are not formally or self-consciously philosophic; they are "natural" philosophers, average citizens of the world who have arrived at a certain view of life which sustains them by providing a touchstone of meaning as to what is God, what is Man or Woman, and what is their own place in the universe.

Jung describes this as his own philosophic attitude in the Prefatory Note to his "Answer to Job." Stressing the subjective urgency of his need to arrive at such a meaning he says:

> The study of medieval natural philosophy—of the greatest importance to psychology—made me try to find an answer to the question: what image of God did these old philosophers have? Or, rather: how should the symbols which supplement their image of God be understood? All this pointed to a *complexio oppositorum*.[63]

Jung shows in this work, as in numerous others, that he must question the basic religious assumption that God exists a priori (in this case, the God of the Old Testament). As the great Jewish scholar, Gershom Sholem, once put it (in a private conversation), Jung starts this work in an exaggerated tone of satire worthy of Voltaire. But his devotion to natural philosophy honors the tradition of those who had no doubt that a God-religion had to be accepted as a basis from which to begin one's study. It has been shown that there is not a single philosophic concept put forth by the pre-Socratic philosophers which is not derived from some previous myth or ritual in early Greek religion.[64] Yet *natural philosophy is not religion*, since it opposes faith in the religious symbols by asserting the higher need to understand them. This understanding, however, may inhibit certain important feelings of trust in life or the operation of humanistic ethical systems. Just as aesthetic sensibility may lead to self-divestiture and preciosity, unchecked philosophizing may be a purely rational quest for the meaning of life, leading to a state of pompous isolation.

I see examples of this in patients whose initial approach to analysis lies in their eagerness to air their views on life in general and impress the analyst, with whom they can discuss their ideas endlessly. The inclination to philosophize, therefore, may become, like the aesthetic tendency in its early phase, a form of resistance to settling down to face the personal problems from which such people are suffering and which have brought them to analysis in the first place. They are so reasonable that one feels there can be no disagreement between them and ourselves as therapists, since we, too, have been taught to be as reasonable and as scientific as possible. Their conflicts seem to find reconciliation in the very act of philosophizing, and it may be hard to recognize how inaccessible they are to psychological change. But these resistances may not be as strong as they seem. Most analysands are usually ready enough to drop them in order to plunge into their own depths.

Occasionally, however, we meet stronger resistances, and then we may have to acknowledge that their ideas have an intrinsic validity which cannot be removed until they are ready to come more closely in touch with individual psychological needs. No one can give up real convictions without considerable psychic shock. Accordingly, such people, usually men with a superior thinking function, need to be allowed to think through this therapeutic challenge to their philosophic attitude before exploring the psyche more deeply.

Actually, in some cases, this preliminary discussion of a philo-sophic nature may not be without depth; in people with trained intelligence it may be a way of understanding psychic phenomena in terms of philosophy itself. It is by no means only men with a superior thinking function who can do this. Intellectually curious men and women of all sorts, who approach everything with a question which requires an answer about the meaning of life and human behavior, are not content with letting the rituals or the myths of human existence speak for them and are looking for their own concealed motives. They often need to understand personality differences, and here we meet Jung's classification of personality types and functions in one of its most convincing forms. Jung himself derived his original theory of extraverted and introverted types from studies in philosophy which describe them as exponents of realism and nominalism.[65] We also see how frequently the philosophy of "being" reflects Jung's idea of the sensation function, while the philosophy of "becoming" suggests very strongly the function of intuition.

 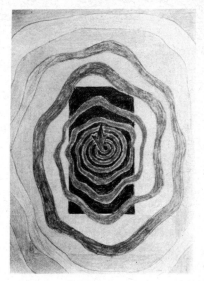

Two colored drawings by author.
(*left*, blue spiral, red center; *right*, red spiral, blue center)

But although Jung described fully the two philosophic opposites historically represented by realism and nominalism, he pointed out that they remain essentially dogmatic unless they can be reconciled with each other; only then do they become philosophy in any true sense. Two kinds of judgment require a third, which is not given unless some reconciling symbol can be found to unite them.

If, in the light of this contribution, we ask again our initial question about the validity of a philosophic attitude, we have some real psychological theory to support us. But we have not explored it in depth. An important contribution to this is to be found in the imaginal activity of the psyche; such activity is often represented in drawings, writings or other art forms by persons undergoing analysis. This occurs spontaneously and it is a surprise to the individual who produces this imagery to learn from his therapist that it contains a philosophic meaning. This was my own experience once in an early period of my analysis with Jung. I drew two pictures with colored pencils, one in blue and one in red. Both had the same spiral design with a structural design in the background, in one case a yellow star and in the other a square blue field. The blue spiral sprang from a red center; the red spiral from a blue center.

When I showed these two drawings to Jung he surprised me by saying, "Yes, philosophy is also a way." From this I learned to understand that the philosophy he referred to was that aspect of Taoist philosophy that is symbolized by the t'ai chi symbol with its dynamic interaction of yang and yin.

☯

It is difficult to describe this imaginal activity without seeming to make it appear either more important or less important than it really is. The images themselves may seem highly colored and exciting or soberly and economically abstract. Synchronistic or parapsychological experiences may occur to people engaged in this activity, but since, in using this method, they must maintain their own personal identity as participant-observers throughout, they are even more than normally protected from hallucinatory invasions. In other words, they must continually humanize and relate personally to their visionary experiences, and in this lies the therapeutic value of such a method. Its philosophical implications can be understood only after the experience has passed. The immediate psychic situation has been revealed and can be explored later for deeper or higher meanings. This creates a kind of movement whereby the original statement repeats itself on a more advanced plane.

Imaginal activity provided the basis for what Jung called active imagination. It is frequently discussed in relation to art therapy, an example of which I gave above in writing of the aesthetic attitude. But the images appropriate for illustrating a philosophic attitude have a different character from those associated with art or religion. There are two main themes which recur in this context, a creation myth and the myth of the divine number.[66] In the first case, that of a creation myth, I have observed that people often identify this mythologem with a sense of recreating the world, their world, anew. It is a return to the source of life, a return to the most primitive conception of godhead, the primal self-image of which is Father Sky and Mother Earth lying in an eternal embrace. This original unity is thought to be disrupted by the appearance of a culture-hero who must separate the original parents, thus creating out of unity a duality. A good example is the Melanesian myth of creation in which Tane was such a hero-figure;[67] he placed his head and shoulders against Mother Earth and with his feet pressed against Father Sky, pushed and pushed until they were parted, placing

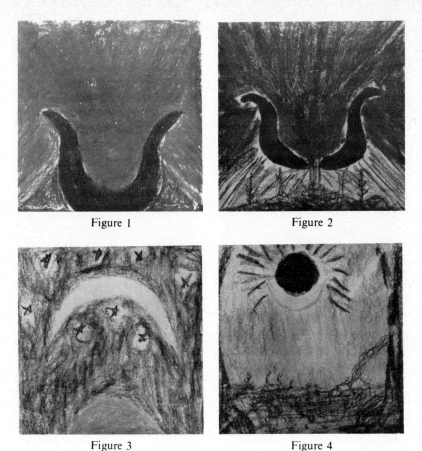

Figure 1

Figure 2

Figure 3

Figure 4

Mother Earth below and Father Sky aloft. All nature could then for the first time come into being and with it mankind could grow and flourish.

Four pictures in a single series (above) drawn by a woman patient of mine illustrated this type of cosmogonic myth, beginning with the original at-oneness of earth and sky, which she expressed as a symbolic containment of sun held on earth in a great vessel. Next she represented the separation of earth from sky and between them the creation of life on earth. This was followed by a picture of moon and stars, which defines a further separation of opposites—day from night. In the fourth picture there was a reassemblage of all

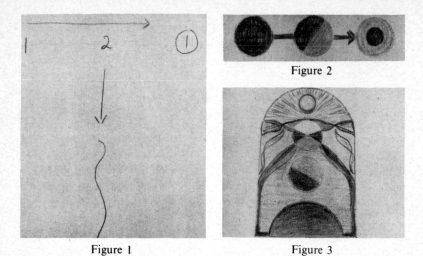

Figure 1   Figure 3

these elements, composing a final balance of two pairs of opposites, earth and sky, sun and moon, with the human family as the center, influenced by a sun-moon conjunction above, and supported by the green earth below.

By way of answer to this woman's stated problem—that of a split between spirit and nature dictated by her religious training—her fantasy creates a primal union of opposites, then a separation followed by a reconciliation of opposites. This inclusion of a previously rejected principle in this woman's religious attitude, an earth religion in accordance with a seasonal birth-death-rebirth cycle, then produces a cosmogonic symbol of wholeness in which the opposites, male-female, spirit-nature, are integrated in a satisfying pictorial design. This is one person's humble version of an archetypal theme which echoes, without her knowing it, some of the great cosmogonies of ancient times.

The story of creation has a kind of internal rhythm that obeys at one time a linear and at other times a cyclic motion. The linear aspect is suggested by the significant number symbolism of the four pictures with their origin in primal unity, separation into two, then an implied, transcendent third, followed by the fourth that rounds out the full conjunction of opposites. One could easily have failed to notice the role played by number symbolism in this series, but it became the central theme in another series of imaginal pictures

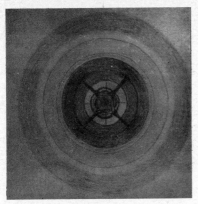

Figure 4   Figure 5

(shown on these two pages) drawn by a man with a problem similar to the woman's, a split between spirit and nature. In his case it was also expressed as a split between thinking and feeling, as psychological functions of the personality. The philosophic nature of his series was made clear by the fact that the movement consisted of number symbolism alone, without reference to any mythologem. Here the creation myth was absorbed in the play of natural numbers as they alone created this man's myth of meaning. It might be said that his fantasy illustrated what von Franz tells us is now true for the physicist, Heisenberg, who imagines that only in mathematical forms can the future physicist denote the elementary particles of matter as "representation of a whole series of symmetry characteristics."[68] Noting that such a closed mathematical schema "is today once again far from realization," von Franz points out the following highly significant fact:

> We discover that the whole structure of mathematics itself and with it all the equations used by the physicist in the investigation of matter are based on an irrational just-so datum, that is, on *the series of natural whole numbers* ... and cannot be derived from anything beyond themselves. So we are again faced with an ancient God-image, that of the Pythagoreans![69]

Number symbolism has its rational meaning in the fact that imaginal activity can be shown to resort to numbers in order to awaken a primordial response as an answer to *a specific, individual problem*. We may then expect to find, as my patient did, a symbolism illustrating von Franz's statement that "the archetypes are given to manifesting themselves in an 'ordered sequence,' of which the number series forms, as it were, the most primitive expression."[70]

Now, there appears to me to be a strong intellectual objection to this idea that numbers represent the most primitive appearance of archetypal motifs. If they are "just-so," naturally whole, and not to be reduced to anything else, who is going to make this symbolism understandable and assimilable to consciousness? Should we not stop thinking about meanings and simply rely on music or dance to satisfy our experience of the archetypes as "ordered sequence"? The answer to this is an integral part of my thesis here that only a philosophic attitude can make sense of such symbolism. This manifestation of the archetype requires a *logos* and cannot be content with the aesthetic, the religious or the social attitudes to explain it.

For those whose primary cultural attitude is one of these others, especially if it is the social attitude, the philosophic attitude must seem irrelevant if not actually obscurantist. I am sure this must be the reaction many people have to von Franz's work and I had a personal experience of this when I presented the material of these patients at a public lecture to a group of people supposedly interested, above all, in philosophy. This surprised me especially because I thought I had made it clear that my above-mentioned patients, both the woman and the man, were *personally* motivated to find the meaning of number symbolism to help them with a very human condition of psychic disharmony. But because I did not fill this out in an array of dramatic behavior patterns, my presentation was, perhaps for them understandably, obscure. I meant to indicate how a *logos* may spring from the archetype itself in response to a person in whom a philosophic attitude is sufficiently developed, and then it may be ready to become a psychological perception later.

Neither of my patients had any doubt as to the therapeutic effect of their imaginal activity, and they were both far enough along in their psychological evolution to know how easy it might be to try to live in the philosophical realization of their problem and to resist translating it into some real change of a psychological nature. The woman, especially, complained how often in the past she had dreamed or fantasized colorful mythologems without any appreciable change resulting in her life. At this time, both she and the man were in a mid-life crisis where the crucial, absolutely necessary change was *only* to be found in a change of philosophical attitude.

The true story of how a philosophical attitude in this "natural" sense becomes translated into psychological terms will be found below in my discussion of the psychological attitude, but I would like to present an introduction to it here.

The drawings of my male patient were either pure whole numbers or simple colored forms to represent them. There was no direct reference to any creation myth, yet the rounding-out of his series in a fifth drawing of the mandala-type showed that a creational cycle existed along with (or as an outcome of) his evolutionary progression of numbers as in Figure 3. Thus he shows two alternating designs: the one an evolutionary progression through the material world to a state of transcendent autonomy, the other a condition of containment in a spiritually centered, self-sufficient mandala design. We have already seen something of this symbolism in the section on the religious attitude, but here I should like to carry it on with further amplification.

F.M. Cornford tells us these two principal patterns were described by the Greek philosophers, who spoke of "the evolutional and the creational":

> In the one, the world is born and grows like a living creature; in the other, it is designed and fashioned like a work of art. ... This evolutionary tradition culminated in the Atomism of Democritus towards the end of the fifth century. ... The alternative pattern, preferred by Plato, for moral and religious reasons, is the creational. The world is like a thing not born but made, containing evidences of intelligent and intelligible design. ... Neither he nor Aristotle believed that the cosmos had any beginning in time or will ever come to an end.[71]

If he were thinking purely philosophically, the analysand would have to choose one or the other of these cosmogonic patterns and be prepared to defend it against a possible attack from those who are convinced of the truth of the other. Psychologically he does not have to make such a choice; he can accept them both as part of a series, and indeed he must do so.

The pictorial progression of the male analysand described above ended, as I have said, with a fifth stage represented by a drawing. From von Franz we learn that number sequences may be found "in

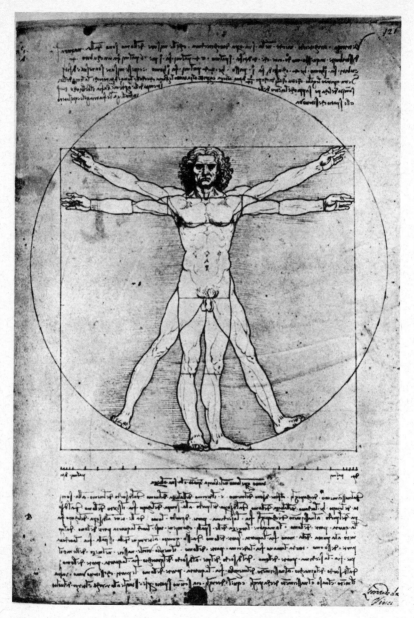

Proportions of the Human Figure—Leonardo da Vinci

rhythmical configurations of the number four" which seek to define a primal origin and an ultimate goal. The movement between these is represented archetypally as linear or as circular but it always returns or goes forward to the number one. In our man's series the original unity therefore became five in a circular model. This process is described in the alchemical axiom of Maria Prophetissa: "The one becomes two, the two becomes three, the three becomes the one that is the fourth."[72] Represented graphically, as in my patient's last two drawings, when the four becomes centered, it indicates that there should be a fifth element in the center of the four-sided square or the graduated circle. This was known in alchemy as the *quintessentia* (or essence of the number four) and is at the same time the number one in this context.

Von Franz speaks of five as "the primal one made manifest, and its progressive ordering effect on the hierarchy of numbers is also recognized in the number fifty."[73]

The one, made manifest, is shown with striking effect in the drawing of Leonardo da Vinci of a naked man with limbs outstretched in a circular design where five is the number of appendages to the body, arms, legs and head whereas four is the circular design itself, combined with a square.

Five as the centered four, according to von Franz, "stands at the center of quaternary mandala structures in the Chinese philosophy of numbers, represented by the Ho-Tu and Motu models," each of which represents the movement of ten numbers around a central one which may be five or ten. Hence the number five:

> stands for the element of the earth carrying and centering all things at the foundations of existence. ... It is the principle of the expanding feminine, K'un, which brings the spirit into material and spatial manifestation.[74]

In the progression of numbers from one to five Jung describes a psychological process inherent in each step. As summarized by von Franz:

> At the level of one, man still naively participates in his surroundings in a state of uncritical unconsciousness [cf. my patient at the beginning of treatment] submitting to things as they are. At the level of two, on the other hand, a dualistic world-and-god image gives rise to tension, doubt, and criticism of god, life, nature and oneself. The condition of three, by comparison, denotes insight, the rise of

consciousness and the rediscovery of unity on a higher level; in a word *gnosis* (as knowledge). But no final goal is reached for trinitarian thinking lacks a further dimension; it is flat, intellectual, and ... encourages intolerant and absolute declarations ... this is the reason why in number symbolism three is so often connected with time.[75]

In contrast to three the number four is a timeless representation of a state of primal wholeness to be regained in the course of a mature development of consciousness. Jung has sometimes been called the philosopher of the number four. But if one reads his works in that spirit one would make the mistake of thinking that he is advising us to aim for a goal that is so timeless and eternal that it cannot ever be realized.[76] What he emphasizes most frequently in his writings, as von Franz points out, is that "a psychological problem of considerable importance is constellated between the numbers three and four ... for it is bound up with painful insights":

> In a curiously retrograde manner the number four brings us back to the *unus mundus*. As a consequence of the step [from three] to four our mental processes no longer revolve about intellectual theory, but partake of the creative adventure of "realizations in the act of becoming."[77]

Jung, however, was not content with this as a formulation for individuation as a goal because it would stop the process on too intuitive a level. If everything is in an eternal state of becoming it merely returns upon itself repetitiously and no real change can take place. Philosophy in the psychological sense should bring about real changes in people's actual lives in the world. Hence he recognized the need, following the ancient philosophies, to postulate that quality of the number four that contains the one but carries it forward to a new level of comprehensibility as the number five. As such, it brings about a sense of psychological unity in which an awareness of the Self as the fourth is made specific and individual by the centering power of the *quintessentia*.

The number symbolism I have elaborated above was used as amplification of the imaginal activity of patients shown in their pictorial material. I do not wish to convey the impression that everyone in a process of therapeutic analysis should paint images of their active imagination. Language, or the process of thinking itself, may for many carry the full meaning of what is implied by a philosophic attitude.

As with my descriptions of the other cultural attitudes, I have tried to keep my perceptions close to the archetypal source of the philosophic attitude. This requires a sacrifice of much that could be said to illuminate the range of philosophic attitudes to be found in a larger study of epistemology. The psychological reason for that sacrifice will be more fully apparent in Part Two, where I will continue the earlier discussion of a psychological attitude.

5

Discussion of the Cultural Attitudes

Anyone who has understood and accepted my description of the four attitudes, and can support my thesis that a psychological attitude may also find its place among them, will require no further discussion. However, I am mindful of the difficulties some people had in accepting these postulates when I first presented them in 1962.[78] They asked: What cultural forms besides mine had been proposed by other students of culture? Why had I chosen these four attitudes and why only four? Why not include a scientific attitude? What relevance, if any, did I think the four attitudes had to Jung's four functions of the personality? What historical origin did I ascribe for the appearance of four cultural attitudes? I propose to answer these questions briefly in the order I have listed them.

I have found valuable support outside my own psychological discipline among certain friends and colleagues who liked my exposition of the attitudes and felt no need to intellectualize it. A similar type of acknowledgment came from certain writings which fell into my hands at the right time to encourage me. The best of these was Irwin Edman's *Four Ways of Philosophy*, which he presents in four chapters entitled "Logical Faith," "Social Criticism," "Mystical Insight," and "Nature Understood." I found here many points of likeness to my cultural attitudes; specifically, *logical faith* corresponds to my philosophic attitude, *social criticism* to the social attitude, *mystical insight* to the religious attitude and *nature understood* to the aesthetic attitude.

I found a similar way of viewing culture among French anthropologists, as described by Claude Lévi-Strauss in his beautifully worded essay, "The Scope of Anthropology." The French anthropologists rescued anthropology from Durkheim's reduction "of all culture to one total social fact,"[79] just as Jung rescued psychoanalysis from a similar reductive interpretation of culture based on the sexual theory of neurosis established by Freud. Lévi-Strauss describes this new attempt to rehabilitate a differentiated picture of culture:

> Now, this analysis in depth was to permit Mauss, without contradicting Durkheim ... to reestablish bridges—which at times had

72

been imprudently destroyed—between his concern and the other sciences of man: history, since the ethnographer deals in the particular, and also biology and psychology. ... Too often since Durkheim—and even more among some of those who believe themselves to be liberated from his doctrinal grip—sociology had seemed like the product of a raid hastily carried out at the expense of history, psychology, linguistics, economics, law, and ethnography. To the booty of this pillage, sociology was content to add its own labels; whatever problem was permitted to it could be assured of receiving a prefabricated "sociological" solution. ... Social facts do not reduce themselves to scattered fragments. They are lived by men, and subjective consciousness is as much a form of their reality as their objective characteristics.[80]

A social attitude is beautifully characterized in Mauss's affirmation that what is essential in society:

is that movement of all, the living aspect, the fleeting instant in which society becomes, or in which men become, through feeling, conscious of themselves and of their situation vis-a-vis others.[81]

Contrary to the sturdy, pragmatic assertions of sociologists, any attempt to pin down this "living aspect" of social reality, writes Lévi-Strauss:

will remain largely illusory: we shall never know if the other fellow whom we cannot, after all, become, fashions from the elements of his social existence a synthesis which can exactly correspond to that which we have worked out.[82]

As Lévi-Strauss indicates, we may use other cultural attitudes to form those symbolic bridges which are necessary for communication, one of which is an aesthetic attitude. This has led the anthropologists to create a science of *semiology*, which, in the sense that Ferdinand de Saussure employed it, includes language, myth, "the oral and gestural signs of which ritual is composed, marriage rules, kinship systems, and certain terms and conditions of economic exchange."[83] This all depends upon aesthetic apperception and in studying these behavior patterns the anthropologist himself acquires on the one hand an aesthetic detachment from the culture he studies, and on the other a special kind of empathy with it. In the first case, the field worker views the primitive society he has come to study as a symbol of something which is predetermined by his own Western education, and he tends to see this image as part of a universal pattern, without antecedents but maintaining a mysterious correspondence to other forms in other places, regardless of diffusions of custom or evolutionary change.

In contrast to this kind of aesthetic apperception, with its detachment from the objects or persons of its study, we find those field workers who immerse themselves so thoroughly in the mythology and ritual of small societies that they almost become psychically identical with them. This may lead certain enthusiasts into grotesque forms of aesthetic imitation. Sometimes, however, it leads anthropologists to genuine initiatory experiences in the societies they have come to study, as we see in Carlos Castaneda's account of his shamanic apprenticeship, *The Teachings of Don Juan: A Yaqui Way of Knowledge*, and its excellent Jungian interpretation by Donald Williams.[84] The value of this is found in a projective identification which, in the right circumstances, creates the mood for acquiring subjective insights which may correspond to objective facts. At its best, it enables Lévi-Strauss to say:

> Our science arrived at maturity the day that Western man began to see he would never understand himself as long as there was a single race or people on the surface of the earth that he treated as an object.[85]

Then, leaving the aesthetic attitude abruptly, he adds, "It was to spread humanism to all humanity."[86]

Humanism, as I have come to understand it psychologically, comes from a special blend of religious and social attitudes. As Christianity lost its hierarchical structure and became broadly socialized, from the time of the late Renaissance in Europe, religion became anthropocentric as well as theocentric. Lévi-Strauss speaks of the

> very exceptional emotion which the anthropologist experiences when he enters a house in which tradition, uninterrupted for four centuries, goes back to the reign of Francis I . . . especially how many ties link him with that age in which the New World was revealed to Europe by being laid open to ethnographical inquiry![87]

He therefore deplores the fact that it has taken so long for anthropology to be recognized, but this is so because the heavy hand of colonialism prevented the men of earlier times from recognizing the authenticity of the primitive societies. Only with the approach of the modern era in which we are still living was pure anthropology born. The first characteristic of this, as Lévi-Strauss rightly asserts, "is of a philosophical order":

> As Merleau-Ponty has written, each time the sociologist (but it is the anthropologist he is thinking of) returns to the living sources of his knowledge, to that which operates in him as a means of understanding the cultural formations most remote from himself, he is spontaneously indulging in philosophy. . . . And, indeed, the field research with which every anthropological career begins is the mother and wet-nurse of doubt, the philosophical attitude par excellence. The "anthropological doubt" does not only consist of knowing that one knows nothing, but of resolutely exposing what one thought one knew, and indeed one's very own ignorance. . . . I think it is by its more strictly philosophical method that anthropology is distinguished from sociology.[88]

Thus we see that Lévi-Strauss outlines a series of cultural attitudes for anthropology that neatly parallel my clinical observation that these same four attitudes are also basic in general culture: the social, religious, aesthetic and philosophic.

It sometimes seems that Jung's four typological functions, taken separately, subtend the cultural attitudes. In *Psychological Types*, he speaks of two kinds of intuition in an introvert: that which tends toward an aesthetic attitude, and that which inclines one toward a philosophic attitude.[89] In other places, Jung seems to regard aestheticism as the product of the two "perceptive" functions, intuition and sensation, while the philosophic or social attitudes become identified with the two "rational" functions, thinking and feeling.[90]

In his later work, however, Jung disclaims any identity between cultural attitudes and psychological function. In his writings, it becomes clear that intellectual understanding is not the exclusive property of the thinking function. The perceptive functions, intuition or sensation, may provide an approach to art and to some extent may define the style in which an artist paints or writes or composes; but a true work of art, like the successful result of a scientific experiment, stands on its own feet regardless of the personal psychology of its creator or perceiver.

No matter how faithfully we develop the four functions or understand them in other people, they do not account for the existence of religious, philosophic, aesthetic or social values. Hence there is a remarkable difference between people of identical personality type and function if they are differently oriented to culture. This suggests that a prerequisite for psychological maturity lies in attaining cultural maturity no less than in developing one's personality in the context of an individual life situation. But where the personality functions and the cultural attitudes do meet, they form very interesting combinations of what we may call "life-style," as illustrated by Joan Evans in *Taste and Temperament*.[91] I have also pointed out the relevance of Dr. Meiklejohn's view of education as a means of providing such a "listing of cultural groupings" (above, p. 26) as would certainly bring the functions of personality into connection with a wide variety of cultural attitudes.

Nor should the cultural attitudes be confused with vocational ambitions. It has sometimes been assumed that by culture I meant institutionalized cultural forms or the roles people play in expressing them. Thus a social attitude was thought to be equivalent to that of a political reformer or social worker, an aesthetic attitude only embodied in an artist, a philosophical attitude found in a full professor of philosophy, while a religious attitude could be appropriately represented only by the devout member of a church or by a priest or theologian. I use the term "attitude" in a sense that cannot be equated with vocational choices. Any one of the four attitudes may be experienced by anyone, regardless of vocation or personality. One comment that struck me as particularly apt, when I first began to notice cultural attitudes, was made to me in a personal conversation with the religious historian, Frederick Spiegelberg, in which he observed that clergymen, far from always being religious, may be drawn to their calling by aesthetic, philosophic or social interests. One might strive to achieve equal development of all the attitudes; but I think this must be very rare, and possibly not even desirable. The most culturally alive people I know regard themselves as incomplete and are eagerly learning and recombining new attitudes all their lives with all the limitations of time in this respect. (*Ars longa, vita brevis.*)

In choosing and describing these four cultural attitudes I am well aware that I may be open to the criticism of being unwilling to subject my views to a rigorous scientific critique. It has been suggested, for instance, as already mentioned, that I should have included a scientific attitude in my list. I hope my previous exposition shows why I did not do so, and that, in keeping my fourfold classification of attitudes as it is, I was not trying to burden analytical psychology with still another set of "four functions." Therefore, I repeat: So far as we know, the functions of the personality are, by definition, found to be psychologically constant whereas the cultures themselves are in a continual process of change and reformation. Furthermore, I consider that a scientific attitude is not primary but is a hybrid combining two other attitudes, which it also increasingly shares with them: the philosophic and the aesthetic. Two of the greatest originators of science, Aristotle and Descartes, were imbued with a philosophic attitude by which they sought to limit man's subjectivity to a minimum in observing the nature of man or God. A similar kind of objectivity was made possible by the adoption of an aesthetic attitude allowing certain men to stand aside from life and from themselves, observing nature and man from a significant distance. Starting from this aesthetic attitude they have, like Leonardo da Vinci, made remarkable discoveries of a scientific nature.

I do recognize, however, that there is something unique in any evolved scientific attitude, which is neither philosophic nor aesthetic but only itself, and it is precisely this sense of uniqueness that we also find in the psychological attitude which animates the heuristic method of our present study. It may be that this method will reveal not only the existence of a psychological attitude but that of a scientific attitude of which the psychological is a part. But certainly, because of their so very recent appearance in history, we cannot claim for science or psychology the same epistemological authenticity that we can demonstrate in the four basic cultural attitudes as they originated and grew out of history into their contemporary forms. There is some evidence of their original unity in primitive societies that have resisted technological development. Although absolutely pure cultures no longer exist, we can reconstruct many of the tribal chantways or dance-dramas from ceremonials still in use, where, far from the urban centers of civilization, they still maintain some of their original integrity. If we were to attend a Navaho healing ceremonial, or a Bushman rain dance, an Australian initiation rite or an Eskimo hunting ritual, we would find that the meaning of the entire culture is evoked in each one.

Such ceremonies are religious because they invoke the presence of gods or demigods, mediated by a priest or medicine man. The rites are social because the physical health and social well-being of the individuals or the tribe are intimately bound up with them. All the adults, and frequently the children, participate actively in the rites to ensure both their food supply and their spiritual welfare. Everything has its place in the family groups of the food-gathering peoples, and in the totemic groups of the hunters, planters and herdsmen. The rites are aesthetic by virtue of their performance of dances in costume, accompanied by music or drumming, and primitive people frequently leave records of this dance-drama, or pre-figure it in rock-drawings, carvings and in sand or pollen paintings of incomparable artistic merit. Finally, they are philosophic in the sense that different strands of tribal lore are woven together to provide a rational explanation of the origin of the rites embodied in a creation myth. This explains the cosmos, the evolution and present place of animals and men living within it together, according to theory. I have tried to expose the continuing presence of cultural attitudes today in accordance with these probable origins.

PART TWO

A PSYCHOLOGICAL ATTITUDE

The rose window of Notre Dame Cathedral, Paris.

6

Dualities of the Self

Jung's opus, apart from his scientific contribution to modern psychology, is one gigantic amplification of the archetypes of the unconscious and cannot, as such, be considered only psychological. Amplification is a means, not an end. Only after amplifying the archetype as fully as seems appropriate in each case do we become psychologists, able to test the amplifications to find where, specifically, they apply to you or me or the ethnic tradition in which we are rooted. What we recognize as traditional culture-forms, and treat as amplification for dreams and fantasies, can be experienced purely culturally, whether aesthetically, socially, philosophically or religiously, whereas a psychological attitude depends upon a specificity of consciousness that can single out from any amplification the one realization that applies to a particular individual at a particular time in his or her life.

A woman patient of mine had a dream in which a bear with a woman's dress danced around the dining room of her mother's house in a manner that was frightening but also invigorating if she held her own ground. On a personal level of interpretation the dream had to do with this woman's sense of holding her own ground in a new way in relation to her mother. The bear dance, however, expressed this in a way that suggested an initiation ritual. I happened to know a good deal about the bear as an archetypal image, hence I was able to amplify the woman's dream and interpret it much more effectively and with specific reference to her psychological need for understanding.[92]

For this kind of scholarship the method of natural science becomes necessary in the sense that any psychological theory must be judged in terms of its applicability, and the method of amplification is more truly applicable to a demonstration of archetypal imagery than any other. This may be seen most clearly in *Symbols of Transformation*, Jung's first full-length demonstration of this method, even before he knew it was to become a method. In this exploration of a woman's published dreams and fantasies, he had no personal associations from the patient to help him, and he drew upon mythology for their equivalent. Without even knowing

81

her, he arrived at the correct diagnosis of her case, as was later verified by her psychiatrist. This may not seem like a remarkable feat today, but it was unheard of in 1912.

New discoveries are either misunderstood or misused, and Jung's early work suffered this fate, leading some practitioners—and even Jung himself at times—to adopt the method of amplification without bothering to keep it within its true context or to apply it to a specific individual. Hence, they used the mythological images to weave tapestries with aesthetic appeal, or they wrote essays with philosophical conclusions which could never be scientifically verified. That is why I have taken such pains to define social, religious, philosophic and aesthetic attitudes so that they may amplify but not obscure the psychological truth to be demonstrated. Only in that way, if at all, can we reveal the nature of a psychological attitude existing in its own right.

Whoever works by amplifying the material, and then specifying its relevance for each individual case, will notice, as Jung did, that the unconscious autonomously produces symbols of a unifying center that effectively compensate states of psychic dissociation. The Tibetan mandala is the most convincing form, and Jung adopted this image as a general representation of psychic centering. But there is another centering symbol which has not received the notice it deserves. This comes to light in dream material, and it is abundantly illustrated in Mircea Eliade's studies in comparative religious symbology.[93] This is a vertical design, or *axis mundi*, represented as linear or curvilinear, appearing in such different images as tree, rope, ladder, steeple, minaret or stupa and in the erect human body with its symmetry ordered in relation to the spinal column. In contrast to this vertical design we have the mandala-form, with its circular character, represented by spiral or labyrinthine or shell-like designs, round objects, sacred stones, caldrons, burial mounds, circular tombs, domes, squares, orbs, sun circles, moon rings or the sacred eye. Just as the vertical designs have been elaborated to form ziggurats, church spires or minarets, so the mandala design may become the dome, the rose window or the ground plan of any sacred precinct. Clearly, both designs may therefore coexist.

I have been chiefly interested in collecting from my own dreams and those of my patients examples of a tendency to join or unify these two forms of centering (e.g., above, p. 30), and then to try to unearth their secret meaning, because I think they help us to unify symbolically any two cultural traditions which normally stand in opposition to each other.

In the earlier discussion of the philosophic attitude, I indicated that these two traditions may be represented by the "evolutionary" and "creational" respectively, and showed the special personal relevance of this idea in a man's active imagination. The image corresponding to one case was developmentally alive in a perpetual process of becoming, while in the other case the image was so perfectly self-contained that it suggested a permanent state of being. In their religious form these images represent the incandescent experience of spiritual reality (e.g., as in resurrection fantasies) or the experience of the immanent god in nature (e.g., as in rebirth fantasies). So many examples have been reported by Jungian writers besides Jung that I need not repeat them extensively. But it *is* necessary to point out here in greater historical detail something about the resolution of the conflict that inevitably occurs when these two traditions, the evolutionary and the creational, meet without any mediation.

According to theory, there is the essentially unknown influence of the Self as the central archetype. Jung describes the ego's right attitude toward the Self as having "no definable aim or visible purpose."[94] What initially promotes a tendency to seek an intelligible goal is our egoistic identification with whatever religion, philosophy, art form or social organism influenced us from early years and therefore became an ego-ideal. In the process of conscious individuation this preformed structure becomes inadequate, so that the personality, instead of being supported or enriched by it, feels isolated or abandoned. Then the individual may conceive an original image existing independent of previous cultural influence, which becomes the true model or symbol of what he or she hopes to realize. Such a symbol precludes the exclusive use of known culture forms; it has come into being from an intensely personal experience, but cannot be traced to any known categories of experience or knowledge. It is unique. Hence I think we are allowed to call this kind of symbol psychological in the truest meaning of the word; it makes possible *specific knowledge of the nature of the human psyche.*

The cases reported in my *Thresholds of Initiation* led me to formulate a number of archetypal stages of development corre-

sponding to rites and ceremonials to be found in tribal societies and
in the higher religious systems. These stages were represented on
one hand by a progressive period of adaptation—first to the
mother-world, then to the father-world and then to the social
group. I found that in a therapeutic transference to me these
patients tended to recapitulate the stages of development in
significant ways, as if to review and repair damage done by faulty
parenting or teaching at an early age. But they did not begin at the
parental level. They regressed to an earlier level where a primal self-
image seemed to precede all memories of past conditioning and to
express an inherent sense of unity which had existed before the
emergence of ego-consciousness. The visual recreation of this
center recorded changes in consciousness or behavior corresponding to the transformation of the primal self-image into cultural
forms accessible to an emerging ego. As successive images of
development they appeared as trickster, hero and, finally, the true
initiate.

On the other hand, when initiation into a peer group had taken
place satisfactorily, I spoke of a "rite of vision" in which the
spontaneous appearance of some form of guardian-spirit bore
witness to the existence of the Self which did not represent any
return to primal unity but seemed to project a religious goal into the
future. This seemed to create individual identity outside parental
influence or group solidarity. I called the image of this goal the
ultimate Self, as distinct from the *primal Self*. Since then, I have
found more evidence for thinking that these two aspects of the Self
are less like images than like two magnetic fields which draw ego-
consciousness up and down, backward and forward, according to
factors associated with age and experience.

The movement between these two archetypal energies may
account for the alternation between regression and progression so
commonly observed during psychotherapeutic treatment. In fact,
such a movement may represent the energic basis of all psychic
reality. If so, it can be visualized not merely as a series of stages like
a stairway between a lower and a higher self-image, but as a circle
embracing them all in a kind of circumambulation. In a diagram,
reproduced here, I represented the coexistence of both the linear
stages of development and the cyclic mode of awareness. The stages
of initiation appear to correspond to a procession of tribal rites,
while the cyclic form of initiation is analogous to the shaman's

"magic flight" into paranormal states of consciousness beyond the experience of ordinary consciousness. Although I had anticipated a possible union of these opposites, I could not at that time understand the larger truth embodied in the symbolic union which I now believe takes place between the linear and cyclic images, or between the evolutional and the creative forms of individual development.

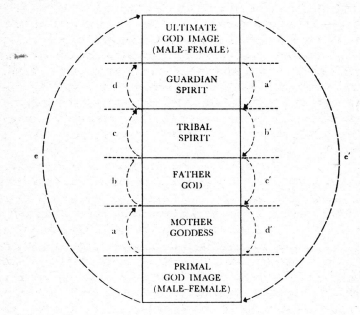

In the development of Jungian theory we have come a long way from Jung's earliest formulation of his analytical method. His own revisions of that first period bring us to this kind of realization as a growing point. Jung had originally stated that his form of analysis should start with a reductive analysis, following the Freudian model of analyzing childhood memories or their still-existing behavior patterns as fixations. Analysis should then proceed to deal with new material in a teleological spirit furthering the development of latent possibilities. We have long known how to modify this definition of methodology by recognizing that we cannot separate the two modes artificially, the reductive method from the prospective method. Now I think we can go further and state that both reductive and prospective methods are pure illusion when it comes to the real task of unifying the opposites. The analysand and the analyst are always moving between the dual energies we call the Self. At one time we seem to be furthering a regression to the infantile or prenatal experience of the primal Self; at another, we are following the psyche's own movement of progression toward some understanding of final things, the ultimate Self.

When we are in harmony with the primal Self we can appreciate our hereditary connection with the ancestors and the beauty of the death-and-rebirth archetype. Although we may be thus meaningfully oriented to the past, this experience can easily become unduly absorbing and repetitive. Erich Neumann has expressed this very well as "source mysticism," which is "dominated by the archetypes of the uroboros and the Great Mother, with which are associated a childlike ego ... and we call yearning to return to this stage "uroboros incest'."[95]

The real turning point between a primal self-awareness and an ultimate self-awareness seems to correspond to Jung's observation that the psyche tends to change its course at the onset of the second part of life, which typically comes between the ages of thirty-five and forty. Then a new consciousness dawns with a glimpse of something beyond—certainly beyond early conditioning. This feels like an opening into the future made possible by having assimilated the essential meaning of one's experience of past ancestral lives if one has the strength of one's conviction. By making this turning point wholly real, one is able to move in that direction, but it does not mean cutting off the other. Depending on where people are at any given time they can, at this stage, turn around and look back or turn and look forward. Consciousness at this turning point is frequently troubled and confused until it gets used to accepting that retrospective and progressive views are not mutually exclusive but can be realized as part of a continuum.

This outlines the possibility of orienting oneself to a primal Self and to an ultimate Self, without experiencing a sense of dissociation between the two. My idea is that the Self is there as the given condition of the archetypal background of all consciousness, and of course we can know nothing about its intrinsic nature, as Jung has told us. But, as individuals with a psychological attitude, we can orient and reorient ourselves to the primal Self and its "eternal recurrence of all things," or to the ultimate Self and its presentiment of final things in a mystery to be revealed beyond imagining. That is why in so many accounts of the Mysteries, it is symbolized as pure light.

Erich Neumann sums up this line of reasoning by contrasting mysticism of the "source" with "last stage" mysticism. He says:

> In contrast to uroboros mysticism which says, "Make me free from selfhood," a fit prayer for world-transforming mysticism (of the last stage) might be, "Fill me with my selfhood. . . ."
>
> This process is accompanied by another in which one might say the world becomes transparent. ... Now neither the extravert's outward vision of the world nor the introvert's inner vision remains in force but a third type of vision arises. What in the primitive stage was realized as an unconscious bond and mixture between ego and non-ego returns now on a higher level as the possibility of symbolic life.[96]

7

Psychology in Historical Context

If we are to speak intelligibly about the existence of a psychological attitude we must be able to connect it to some extent with our own philosophical tradition, as I indicated in the previous chapter on the philosophic attitude. Here we may recall the period of Western philosophy from which it originates and where we may find some anticipation of our model. This is entirely in line with the tradition that modern psychology does appear to have arisen from philosophy. In most European universities psychology has always been taught in the department of philosophy.

Cornford takes up this theme in his posthumous work, *Principium Sapientiae,* where he finds an important signpost for our modern age in his discovery of a connection between philosophy and shamanism. The philosophic ability to transcend conceptually our human condition has a very ancient, primary place of origin. It is found in the man whose knowledge of truth is what he remembers (anamnesis), and whose capacity to foretell the future (prophecy) is the goal of his endeavor. The one who remembers the truth is the poet who tells the story of creation and who brings the basic cosmogonic myth up to date for one's time. The gift of prophecy is found in the "seer," which was early recognized by Democritus:

> "The wise" in fifth century Greek would include poets and seers as well as sages and philosophers . . . and would connect with the inspiration of poet and seer the philosophic intuition which Democritus called "true born wisdom.". . . Democritus prayed that he might meet with favorable spectres of the gods, who could affect man for good or evil and reveal the future in dreams.[97]

Furthermore, the poet and the seer may not be separate persons, but the same person—he who experiences "mantic inspiration," a form of inspired madness, which, as Homer tells us, endowed the seer Calchas with knowledge of past, present and future. This can also happen to a highly rational philosopher:

> Throughout the conversation in the *Phaedo* on the day of his death, Socrates is to be thought of as inspired with a "mantic" wisdom which sees beyond the confines of rational disputation and he ascribes his power to Apollo.[98]

88

But there is a second form of prophetic madness which is the gift of Dionysus:

> Divination here is concerned with the past and present. It is exercised to discover the "ancient Wraths" of offended spirits whose vengeance has caused hereditary maladies and afflictions. Prophetic madness reveals the means of "deliverance" and "absolution from present evils," having recourse to prayers and service to the gods in rites of purification and initiation. . . . .Initiatory madness . . . introduces many terms associated with cathartic procedure both in medicine and the mysteries.[99]

These initiatory experiences are "not so much to unveil the future as to discover in the past those forgotten errors of which present evils were the consequence." One way to achieve this is through the physician's, or as we might say today, the physician-analyst's or psychotherapist's art in revealing "the hidden present" for cathartic purposes.

A third form of madness, writes Cornford, is:

> "a possession by the Muses," which, seizing upon a tender, virgin soul, rouses it to ecstasy in song and poetry, marshalling countless deeds of men of old for the instruction of posterity. . . . As a man among men, the poet depends on hearsay; but as divinely inspired he has access to the knowledge of an eye-witness, "present" at the feats he illustrates. The Muses are, in fact, credited with the same mantic powers as the seer, transcending the limitations of time. . . .
>
> So Hesiod begins with Muses, who tell of things present, past, and future—the same words in which Homer described the mantic gift of Calchas the seer. And what the Muses reveal to the poet's vision is the origin of the world and the birth of the gods.[101]

The prototype of the "seer-poet" or "prophet-poet-sage" of Cornford's study is then shown to be the aboriginal shaman. The importance of shamanism is that it provides the evidence that there is a primordial root for all true philosophic attitudes. The shaman receives his knowledge and experiences his calling without cultural mediation during a period of psychic sickness, usually around puberty, and from then on is among those whose mediumistic perceptions are directly inspired from the unconscious. This shamanic talent appears in men whose names are also associated with the heights of philosophic rationality. Such a man was Pythagoras. Even the materialist philosopher Epicurus recognized the faculty of the mind which "strains and projects itself far and wide," and the infinite space "to which intelligence yearns to look forward, and which the free projection of the mind traverses in its flight."[102]

The mind "in flight" is more than an apt metaphor for shamanism, with its capacity for archetypal remembrance, its revelation of the hidden present and the shaman's "magic flight," during which he is supposed to leave his earthly body behind for the purpose of exploring spheres of higher consciousness. At the highest level he becomes aware of spiritual fulfillment or ecstasy, which is the goal of yogic detachment. The seer-poet's successor is the philosopher, who is both sophist and lover of wisdom, implying that just as there is a deeper region of the unconscious psyche from which he obtains his initial inspiration, there is also a higher level of consciousness upon which he finds some intimation of immortality.

In order to define the position of the philosopher in relation to the other figures with whom he is related, we might show the origin and development of this figure in a serial form as follows:

shaman—seer—poet—prophet—philosopher—religious mystic

What gives Heraclitus his identity as a philosopher is the *logos* which he found:

> by searching himself; but on the other hand, this wisdom is not the private opinion of Heracleitus, but "common to all.". . . It is in this sense that Heracleitus claims unique inspiration, superseding all poets, prophets, and sages of the past or of his own day.[103]

A recognizable philosopher, writes Cornford, "arguing from point to point and deducting sure conclusions from unquestionable axioms" (and "the first philosopher to offer rigid logical proof instead of making dogmatic pronouncements") was the poet Pareminides, who was concerned not with tangible objects but with metaphysical thought.[104] He made an open confession that the whole of one poem (he wrote in verse) was a revelation to him by a goddess. "However the tradition may have come to him, his journey to, or around, the heavens recalls the heaven-journey (magic flight) of the shaman's ritual drama."[105]

A totally different aspect of philosophy is represented by Empedocles, who seems not to have shared Heraclitus's arrogant contempt for the "learning of many things." His nature, writes Cornford, "was as rich and vital and many-sided as Goethe's, eagerly welcoming every form of experience":

He reproduces with singular completeness every form of Plato's divine madness, every corresponding aspect of his god Apollo and his prototype Orpheus, and sums up in his own person all the characters which he describes as typifying the final, highest incarnation before the return to the divine bliss: seer, minstrel, physician, and leader of men.[106]

This reference to the physician supplies a missing element in the whole series of seer-poet-prophet figures leading up to the philosopher. The shaman is "healer of souls"; he is the blood brother of Hippocrates, the physical physician who later becomes the first true scientist in the ancient world.

Plato's genius lies in the fact that his philosophy extends beyond the Socratic "rational discourse" to the "irrational part of the soul" which is concerned with the recollection of Ideas, "the eternal realities," on the one hand and with the future on the other, with its doctrine of immortality. He is, therefore, in touch with the shaman who "remembers the truth" and with the religious mystic who is in touch with the future which he will perceive in states of ecstasy. Yet he remains the philosopher-poet who remembers the ritual and myths of the origins of culture.

If there was a distinction to be made between the philosopher and the religious mystic, it also exists between the philosopher and the poet. The quarrel between the philosopher and the poet arose from the fact that "there was a common field which both parties claimed for their own."[107] The seer's main concern was to foresee the future, while the poet was occupied with his imaginative vision of the past:

This vision extended backwards to the very beginning of things—the mythical epoch of Hesiod's *Theogony*, the generations of gods before man existed, the succession of divine dynasties, the war of the Olympians and the Titans; and beyond that again, cosmogony, the original formation of an ordered world.[108]

The poets mixed myth and local history freely and indiscriminately; gods and heroes met at localized places and at historically verifiable times, as in Homer, and this shocked the philosophers. "The philosopher's business," writes Cornford, "was to dispel the veil of history or myth and penetrate to the 'nature of things,' a reality satisfying the requirements of abstract thought."[109]

Here again Plato emerges triumphant in this quarrel, since, in the *Timaeus*, he becomes the philosopher-poet who tells the story of creation, in which humankind is no less important than the world of gods. Humankind is the immediate inheritor of myth and, as Heraclitus had said, the true initiator of self-knowledge. In the end, this philosophy becomes an ancient bridge to any modern psychology of the unconscious, stretching between the archetypal world of the ideal images and the human conscious world. In this transition, theocentric myth becomes anthropocentric reality, according to which we can become ourselves without losing touch with our divine heritage.

Thus, in the ancient philosophical tradition there is evidence for the existence of archetypal images in forming our inner conception of our distant past and our immediate future. But ancient man did not therefore dispense with the ritual forms or the mythic images which were a part of his original cultural conditioning, and *no psychology oriented to the individual ever developed out of them in the ancient world.* I emphasize this fact because I find that many modern people have a tendency to look for evidence of individual psychology in cultural traditions where there is only a faint suggestion of what they might like to find in them, so that their quest ends in their own projections without demonstrable evidence to support them.

8

Psychology in Its Modern Context

This brings us to the central question of this part of our study: When did psychology in an individual sense arise? Perhaps we can find indications of some such expression in the Greco-Roman period but I doubt the poets or philosophers of that time were much closer to formulating a psychological attitude than were the early Greeks.

Since we have been following the development of philosophy as our pilot, we cannot help noticing how the spiritual direction of Plato's work was diluted and largely replaced by the materialistic philosophy represented by Aristotle, whose immense influence continued right into the seventeenth century, creating an extraverted philosophy which suppressed any philosophical interest in the existence of an inner life of the soul. However, in the late Middle Ages there still remained a strong introverted position in philosophy represented by *nominalism* as the polar opposite of extraverted *realism*. But philosophy finally may be said to have got stuck in the realist phase and to have largely suppressed the nominalist position, thus preventing further philosophic discussion or any mediation between the two. In his *Psychological Types*, Jung was the first to notice this impasse and to approach it with the kind of insight we expect from a psychological rather than a purely philosophic viewpont.[110]

A good many changes had to take place in the evolution of Western consciousness before this was possible, and the whole story has been told with great sensitivity by L.L. Whyte in *The Unconscious Before Freud*. Without the development of science during the sixteenth, seventeenth and eighteenth centuries Freud and Jung would never have had the incentive to discover the unconscious, and Jung would not have formulated the principle of *psychic energy*, telling us that psychology is not merely "knowledge" of the psyche but the living experience of its consciousness-expanding properties.[111]

Contemporary psychology is no longer what it was when the concept of the unconscious was first introduced by Sigmund Freud. Its formulations since that time have so permeated our culture that

93

we now have assimilated its meaning to a large extent. Gerhard Adler, a leading Jungian, goes so far as to state that the unconscious is no longer useful as a concept.[112] Although I cannot agree with this, it nevertheless points to a fact that the unconscious is not a specific realm where the Platonic models for existence are enthroned in timeless splendor, nor yet a dust bin where we try to throw painful personal thoughts or affects. We need no longer react to the unconscious in the period of Freud but to the unconscious after Jung.

Adler quotes Jung as defining the ego as "a complex datum which is constituted first of all by a general awareness of your body, of your existence, and secondly by your memory data; you have a certain idea of having been *a long series of memories*."[113] Adler then speaks of the paradoxical but highly significant testimony of patients undergoing analysis that "the vision and recollection of the pre-existent pattern, the unconscious wholeness, and of the future possibility, direction, or goal" is exemplified in modern dreams.[114] Inevitably this affords a view of the Self similar to Plato's concept of the inborn memory of ideal images. Adler writes:

> If...we take Plato's concept seriously—and *a fortiori*, Jung's teaching—it would be correct to talk of the Self as the basic and decisive entity and we would so do justice to the fact that whatever we experience through our ego is only an echo or a deviation or an ephemeral configuration of the Self.[115]

It could be argued that this viewpoint simply puts modern psychology back in the nominalist position, from which again to oppose the realist position of extraverted science. But in the light of modern physics and the recognition of a complementarity between the data of physics and the data of analytical psychology, we have reached middle ground between the two from which to envisage a new unity, which L.L. Whyte has explored in *The Next Development in Man*. Our modern situation, as described by Marie-Louise von Franz, is as follows:

> All the great basic themes of the natural sciences are archetypal images . . . that is why Jung emphasized that the collective unconscious is "a perpetual living mirror of the universe." Our subject is "situated between the two antithetical worlds"—the so-called external world open to the senses, and the unconscious psychic substrate which alone enables us to grasp the world at all. . . . If the psychic mirrorings of the material world—in short the natural sciences—

really constitute valid statements about matter, then the reverse mirror-relation would also have to be valid. This would indicate that a quite concrete event in the external world could be understood as a symbolic statement about an objective psychic process, which is conscious to the observer.[116]

Thus Jung created what seems to me the first valid conceptual model for a psychology of the future. Transcending the nominalist or realist positions his model makes possible a psychological attitude that is comprehensive enough to exist in its own right as an essential part of the culture of our time in history.

Reasoning of this kind led Jung to postulate the existence of "absolute knowledge" connected with the archetypal structure of the psyche. This implies a relation of psyche and matter that accounts for certain highly significant synchronistic events where, writes Jung, "it is not always possible to determine whether a primary inner process is accompanied by an outer one, or whether, conversely, a primary outer event is being reflected in a secondary inner process."[117] If one of these seems to cause the other, however, we are dealing not with synchronicity but with parapsychological phenomena where causal, mediumistic interventions occur. True synchronistic experiences can rarely be observed in their entirety but enough of them have been reported to allow Jung to observe that certain "events in the external world. . .have the same *meaning* as endopsychic events."[118] Consciousness of such events is, of course, created by the psyche, a process von Franz significantly calls "self-cognition of the universe."[119] Such "knowledge" comes into a space-time continuum that cannot be measured, but only perceived with a special kind of insight that comes like a revelation.

Occasionally during individual analysis patients who are strongly transferred to the analyst may provide good examples of synchronicity that can be observed with considerably more accuracy than those we hear reported casually. One such case interested me because the same outer event occurred regularly, corresponding to different inner events which, however, all had a similar need to be affirmed and confirmed. This was a woman who would be driving along in her car when certain emotionally toned insights came into her mind with great urgency. This urgency usually had the same quality, namely a wish to accept their positive meaning combined with a strong tendency to doubt them. When in this thoughtful, conflicted mood, frequently stimulated by some recent steps she was about to take in her self-realization in analysis, she would see a license plate on the car in front of her with the numbers seven and eleven in relation to each other. Sometimes it would be 711, sometimes 117, but always the same sense of positive confirmation of the forward-looking aspect of her thought seemed to be emphasized by seeing these numbers.

At first we both were skeptical, rationalizing these occurrences as being purely coincidental or as ideas of reference, which means twisting an outer event or thing to make it correspond to an inner condition; in other words, a delusion. But these events were reported so many times and in relation to so many significant insights that we had to accept them as true synchronicities. One very subtle form of the event which made the insight more meaningful lay in the woman's own association to the number seven as being her individual self or personality, while eleven stood for some more universal sense of Self. When the individual component was predominant the number of the license plate would be 711; when the universal aspect was of greater importance it would be 117. Such precision could not be due to chance, we felt.

If we were to use this example to illustrate what Jung means by absolute knowledge, we could say that just as the psyche may be mirrored in the world, so matter may seem to know itself in the mirror of the objective psyche. But we need to know the conditions under which such experience may become conscious if we are to find anything more in such synchronistic events than their oddity. Actually, the woman's religious problem in her analysis throws some light upon this question. She had a tendency to deny that her quest for mystical self-realization could be achieved in this world or in her lifetime. She did not wish to fall into the position of the uroboric or "source" mysticism referred to by Neumann (above, p. 87), even as she might want to. Only by making her inner life spiritually independent of the world or of outer events could she imagine achieving the spiritual certainty she wanted. Her synchronicities "on the way" all pointed the other way by keeping her active in furthering her worldly vocation, while offering reassurance that she was also spiritually just where she should be.

In this I came to respect the activity of the Self as an ordering principle and was reminded of Jung's emphasis on numbers as "a predestined instrument for creating order, and/or apprehending an already existing, but still unknown, regular arrangement or "orderedness.' "[120] In von Franz's study of numbers we learn that

" 'numerical play' of collective unconscious contents is a symbol for the *unconscious creative urge toward higher consciousness.* It proceeds from the symbol of the Self as the end-image of the individuation process."[121] She also says that "eleven is considered to be the number of the Way of Tao,"[122] and seven, as the number of inner initiation, leads to an apprehension of eleven. That is, the two numbers are intimately related.

A special insight then came to my patient in recognizing that her individual way as represented by seven and the universal Way, as the Tao, could be harmonized instead of being conflicted; the number to express this was nine, suggesting a centered standpoint midway between the two.

Manifestations of the ordering principle in the unconscious, such as this example shows, allow me to encourage others, as well as myself, not to return too often to the "source" of the primal Self, but rather to follow that equally strong movement in the psyche toward higher realizations that seem to invest the symbols of last-stage or ultimate Self with special meaning.

9

Nature and Psyche

The complementarity between physics and analytical psychology that interested Jung in his last years is, as he said himself,[123] more theoretical than actual and although we may admire the intricate patterns of thought inherent in the symbolism of numbers, we may not have much feeling for this approach to the unconscious. But if, instead of physics, we place biology as the complementary opposite of analytical psychology, a more humanly appealing picture emerges and its theoretical justification can be more clearly defined. Instead of contrasting such abstractions as spirit and matter, we then have a more visible pair of complementary opposites which we may call psyche and nature, or when applying this to a human subject we may call them simply soul and body.

Starting with the earliest manifestations of human instinct, we have long known, as the ethologist John Bowlby has demonstrated in *Attachment and Loss*, that the infant responds to some sign from the mother which acts as a stimulus to arouse an innate response to her nurturant capacities. The mother's affective response and the infant's response toward her is hardly more evolved than it is in the higher primates since the biological model postulates the same response for all concerned. We cannot speak of "soul" in this ethological sense, and without some ability to demonstrate the existence of psyche there is no psychosomatic equation, only a more or less complex behavior pattern.

Anthony Stevens, a Jungian analyst and himself a former ethologist, has shown how this kind of study fails to account for the functioning presence of an archetype which endows pure instinct with the value of an emotionally charged image. The psychosomatic equation then states that the behavior pattern gives body to that instinct which looks to the archetypal image for its meaning. Stevens enlarges the ethological view of the mother-child relationship by saying:

> I prefer the Jungian view that the evolving repertoire of behaviors apparent in both mother and child represent stages in the progressive actualization of the mother-child archetypal system . . . associated with subjective experiences in both participants.[124]

He goes on to assert that "archetypal theory permits us to give due weight to the essential loving and intuitive nature of the primal relationship,"[125] and quotes Jung's statement as to how the biological behavioral pole of the equation is enlarged by inclusion of the archetype:

> But the picture changes at once when looked at from the inside, that is, from within the realm of the subjective psyche. Here the archetype presents itself as numinous, that is, it appears as an *experience* of fundamental importance.[126]

Stevens's work is especially valuable in helping us look for some mediating principle between "good" and "bad" images of the primal relationship, and this can be applied to the father archetype or to other forms of relationship experienced numinously for the first time. He says:

> The "object-relations" school, for example, sees them as "introjected" images of the mother in contrary moods. ... Jungians, however, see them as symbolic actualizations of the Good Great Mother and Terrible Mother archetypes respectively.[127]

Our work with patients in psychotherapy is retrospective in that we are never dealing with infants and their mothers at the same time, but children or older people whose complexes stem from that earlier period. As Stevens notes:

> The mother complex ... is no inner reproduction or "videorecording" of the personal mother-out-there, but a product of her interaction with specific phylogenetic components in the child's maturing psyche.[128]

Therefore, since we are dealing with latent memories we are not able to judge the mother objectively but will be dealing with "the archetypal experiences actualized by her,"[129] in the child or adult. (A full picture of the relation of the mother and her child to the primal Self is not relevant here, but may be read with profit in Stevens's ensuing pages.)[130]

An example of a mother complex in a grown man may illustrate what is meant by "archetypal experiences actualized by the mother." This man was easily frightened by women, but he was also normally responsive to their influence and enjoyed pleasing them. But behind his apparently genial disposition, or perhaps because of it, he had built a sort of defense-system to placate them for any discomfort they might feel in his presence, thus warding off any danger to his self-esteem from their negative criticism. I had to ask myself whose negative criticism he had to fear in childhood and of course I assumed it was his mother's. But further information did not reveal her as other than an exceedingly loving mother who bathed her children in the perpetual warmth of her good feeling.

What came to light in his dreams was the image of an archetypal Terrible Mother which told me that his own mother, by her very goodness, had awakened his inner image of a Good Great Mother so strongly that the bipolar nature of the archetype was activated;

Kali—from Mookerjee and Khanna, *The Tantric Way*.

hence the "good" mother-image changed over to the "bad" by way of seeking a balance between the two. Quite simply his fear of women was his fear of this negative aspect of the archetype; his work in analysis taught him how to imagine treating them as human, not as bearers of the archetypal image only. In the end he came to welcome their criticisms when he deserved them. By acknowledging the archetypal image of the Great Mother he then learned to correct a cultural bias by which his mother had embodied the Christian model of the mother who is expected to be the all-loving, compassionate Mary of the Gospels. In the traditional East the Great Goddess was renowned not only for her compassion but also, and more often, for her anger and her impersonal disregard and actual destruction of retrogressive forms of life. This reflects nature with its destruction of dying forms of life followed by regeneration. This nature cycle is horrifically embodied in the figure of Kali as a cultural form of the Great Mother in India.

In chapter three I pointed to the change that has taken place in our culture to provide the image of a more earthy kind of mother than that represented by the Virgin Mary in her medieval aspect as Queen of Heaven (so beautifully represented in the glass window at Chartres called La Belle Verrière). The man mentioned above was greatly helped in reviewing the procession of historical events by which he could place the archetypal aspect of his mother's goodness back where it belonged and free the actual woman both from his projection and her influence upon him. As he withdrew his projection of the archetypal image it actually relieved her of a part of this burden to her identity and it improved their relationship by making it more real.

But what happened, then, to the archetypal *experience*, once he had withdrawn his projection of the image? I trust I have answered this by indicating that he acquired an enlarged view of culture from the resolution of the complex. Typically, this in turn leads to a reassessment of religious history so as to bring this particular cultural image up to date as an individual experience.

The primal experience of mother and child is certainly the most basic form of the psychobiological equation because it cannot exist at all without a fully functioning polarity between the image and the behavior pattern. The experience, as Erik Erikson so rightly observes, establishes in the infant basic trust, from which later to build valid human relationships of all kinds.[131] But as soon as parent-child separation has taken place we may have to experience a wide divergence of the two poles. One may be satisfied while the other is not. Stevens rightly points out that the failure or absence of initiation experiences in our society is due to educational shortcomings or exaggerations.[132] This means that many young boys and girls are unable to find the behavior pattern that would connect them meaningfully with their peers and are left instead with an unsatisfied "initiation hunger." This throws them back upon the image of initiation all the more strongly, from which they must try to extract the courage to grow up meaningfully and only later, with much trepidation, find their place in society. Others are quite well initiated behaviorally by being taken into groups of one sort or other, schools, teams, the armed services or social cliques, but may miss out on the experience of finding their individual identity. But these too, in later life, may hunger for a kind of wisdom like that associated with the Grail quest, and so in our culture many have always responded to that legendary, archetypal journey of inner enlightenment.

There is one type of psychological experience where the chances of finding the right balance between archetypal image and patterned behavior is the most hazardous of all, since it is not caused by mistakes in upbringing or by environmental misadventures. I refer to the universal problem of finding a truly satisfactory love relationship, or, having found it, how to keep it alive. Since so many fail to realize their dreams of love and have to content themselves with compromise solutions, it becomes important to ask how the archetypal content of this instinct behaves subjectively when it cannot be realized.

Literature has no difficulty with this problem. It simply plays over and over the same behavioral theme of a love-death. Whether love or death wins out in the end it is all the same, since a complete outer merging of two personalities in love extinguishes an important part of their individuality; like Paolo and Francesca in Dante's *Inferno,*, they are doomed to float through Hell forever in each other's arms. If they both die, like Romeo and Juliet, their love survives as the eternal promise of some ultimate union to be achieved on a higher plane than could be satisfied in this life by love alone. Edward Edinger has shown, in a brilliant interpretation of *Romeo and Juliet*, that the power of that relationship lies in embodying an alchemical *coniunctio* or union of opposites that does in fact lift this otherwise simple tale of adolescent love to such a height of symbolic meaning.[133] From this point of view any love story only becomes truly meaningful from its archetypal content, not just from its outer manifestation, and the more its outer realization is frustrated, the more significant may be its inner image.

A unique study of this phenomenon from a psychological viewpoint was made by the Jungian analyst Elizabeth Osterman. Because this is not easily available, I will quote from it here at some length and reproduce the drawings of her patient illustrating the process by which an inner conflict may be resolved:

> The tendency for an ordering process to appear spontaneously in the depths of the psyche of an adult under conditions of emotional stress is depicted in a series of drawings done by a patient in an active phase of analysis.
>
> This forty-five-year-old professional woman, a thinking type, had felt she was through with a love life. Suddenly came a bolt of lightning. She unexpectedly fell in love. The drawing in Figure 1 shows how deeply this event hit in the psyche. Only the impregnating fire from the sky and the disturbed primal waters of the unconscious

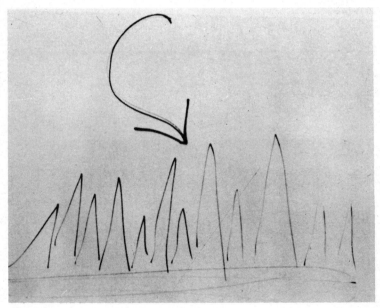

Figure 1

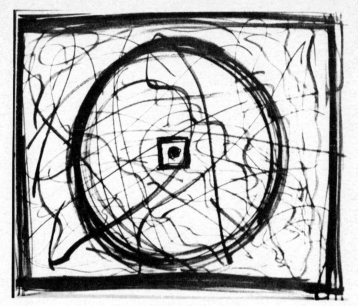

Figure 2

Figure 3

appear. It is reminiscent of the dawn state of the world before living things formed. As Jolande Jacobi has pointed out, "The deeper the unconscious stratum from which the archetype stems, the scantier will be its design, but the more possibilities of development will be contained in it, and the richer it will be in meanings." [*Complex/ Archetype/Symbol in the Psychology of Jung*, p. 56]

The patient pictured the state of confusion into which she had fallen (Figure 2). Her life had suddenly become chaotic, but in the background of the drawing we see the possibility of order and wholeness. Figure 3 shows that she had been hit in the emotional center, in *manipura*. The star overhead indicates it was fated. That this had to do with coming consciousness is suggested by the size of the eye. This embryonic thing is a good image of how undeveloped her capacity was to recognize and to accept her real feelings.

The relationship was not a suitable one for marriage. The patient had to endure a disappointment with much suffering, but in so doing she experienced in depth the realities of her instinctual being. This woman learned in the searing heat of this experience that *needing to be loved* is a polar opposite to being *able to love*.

A year later she pictured the *inner solution* to the problem. A fully formed flower (Figure 4) had grown out of the swamp of unconsci-

Figure 4

ousness. She had become acutely aware of the opposites in her nature and of the energy of their polarity as represented by the two snakes on either side. One points down to the realm of the chthonic, earthy instincts; the other points up to the realm of the spiritual instincts. Between, rooted in the earth, grows the living symbol—the vivid representation of self-realization. Here again is the theme of opposites that become one. Subjectively the patient felt enlivened, rooted in her own nature and at one with herself.[134]

The last, and in many ways the most significant, event we ever have to face archetypally is death. Here there is no question of living the behavior pattern fully, though out-of-the-body experiences of partial death are reported by some people. For most of us, knowledge of death is derived from an archetypal pattern whose total extent can never be experienced as a behavior pattern; the image is present, but the actual experience is withheld. We try to know and yet do not know its essential meaning. However, in all these cases where one must live from the imagined image, and forego acting it out, biology is not absent, since the psychokinetic effect of any strong emotion provides us with a readiness to act or to respond emotionally when the occasion arises.

In this way, even those failures to outwardly satisfy initiation hunger, or love that may not include sexual fulfillment, or the urge toward death that lacks but envisions some form of immortality—even these bring us face to face with the dual nature of the archetype. Acknowledging this, and accepting that as mere humans we are bound to the conflict inherent in duality, we may yet find new life between the opposites of our own nature.

Notes

CW—*The Collected Works of C.G. Jung*

1. Jung, "Analytical Psychology and *Weltanschauung,*" *The Structure and Dynamics of the Psyche,* CW 8, par. 737.
2. Ibid., par. 689.
3. Ibid., par. 713.
4. Erich Neumann, *Art and the Creative Unconscious,* pp. 106-110.
5. Jung, "Analytical Psychology and *Weltanschauung,*" CW 8, par. 689.
6. William James, *Pragmatism: A New Name for Some Old Ways of Thinking,* p. 54.
7. Daryl Sharp, *The Secret Raven: Conflict and Transformation,* p. 103.
8. Victor Turner, *The Ritual Process: Structure and Anti-Structure,* pp. 202-203; see also Turner, *The Forest of Symbols: Aspects of Modern Ndembu Ritual.*
9. Arthur Waley, *The Way and Its Power,* p. 47.
10. See Toni Wolff, "Structural Forms of the Feminine Psyche." Wolff defines four attitudes in women which suggest the social roles they may be called upon to play. They are the Mother, the Amazon, the Hetaera (companion) and the Medium. A good summary of this schema appears in Donald Lee Williams, *Border Crossings: A Psychological Perspective on Carlos Castaneda's Path of Knowledge,* pp. 119-122.
11. Virginia Woolf, *Mrs. Dalloway,* p. 15.
12. See Jung, "The Undiscovered Self," *Civilization in Transition,* CW 10.
13. See Marie-Louise von Franz, "The Process of Individuation," in *Man and His Symbols,* pp. 200-202: "It is no wonder that this figure of Cosmic Man appears in many myths and religious teachings. Generally he is described as something helpful and positive. He appears as Adam, as the Persian Gayomart or as the Hindu Purusha. ...The ancient Chinese, for instance, thought that before anything whatever was created, there was a colossal divine man called P'an Ku who gave heaven and earth their form. ...

    "According to the testimony of many myths, the Cosmic Man is not only the beginning but also the final goal of all life—of the whole of creation. ...

"In our Western civilization the Cosmic Man has been identified to a great extent with Christ and in the East with Krishna or with Buddha."

14. Ibid., p. 203.
15. Jung, *Mysterium Coniunctionis*, CW 14, par. 491.
16. Alexander Meiklejohn, *Education Between Two Worlds*.
17. Ibid., p. 95.
18. Ibid., p. 96.
19. I use Self (capital S) to refer to the archetype of wholeness, the regulating center of the psyche. See Jung, "Definitions," *Psychological Types*, CW 6, pars. 789-791.
20. T.S. Eliot, "The Wasteland," lines 403-404.
21. Edward Edinger, *Ego and Archetype*, p. 186.
22. Paul Tillich, "The Importance of New Being for Christian Theology," in *Man and Transformation*, p. 161.
23. See Mircea Eliade, *The Myth of the Eternal Return*.
24. This dream is dealt with more fully in Joseph L. Henderson and Maud Oakes, *The Wisdom of the Serpent*, pp. 76-77.
25. Aniela Jaffé, *From the Life and Work of C.G. Jung*, pp. 58-59.
26. Ibid.
27. Jung, *Mysterium Coniunctionis*, CW 14, par. 425.
28. Jung, *Psychology and Alchemy*, CW 12, par. 460.
29. Joseph L. Henderson, "Ancient Myths and Modern Man," in *Man and His Symbols*, pp. 141-142.
30. Ibid, p. 141.
31. See Marie-Louise von Franz, *The Problem of the Puer Aeternus*, and Daryl Sharp, *The Secret Raven*.
32. This is discussed at greater length in Joseph L. Henderson, *Thresholds of Initiation*, pp. 33-36.
33. I.M. Lewis, *Ecstatic Religion: An Anthropological Study of Spirit Possession and Shamanism*.
34. Jean Daniélou, "The Word Goes Forth: Christianity as a Missionary Religion," in *The Crucible of Christianity*, p. 284.
35. Ibid., p. 293.
36. Paul Evdokimov, *La Femme et le Salut du Monde: Étude d'Anthropologie Chrétienne sur les Charismes de la Femme*, p. 239. Of John the Baptist, Evdokimov tells us he is violent with the violence of Christ, the prototype for which is the violence found in the figure of Elias (Elijah) of the Old Testament, who was vehement without mercy. This emotional zeal for reform was later tempered

by the gentleness of the Virgin. In an impressive fifteenth-century icon from the school of Moscow, we see Christ seated between two standing figures, the Virgin on one side, John the Baptist on the other, conveying the sense that both are subordinate to the Christ as a symbol of the Self. (See Jung, "Christ, a Symbol of the Self, *Aion*, CW 9ii.)

37. Jean Daniélou, "The Dove and the Darkness in Ancient Byzantine Mysticism," in *Man and Transformation*, p. 277.
38. See Teilhard de Chardin, *Building the Earth*.
39. I am indebted to Marilyn Nagy for acquainting me with this tradition.
40. Daniélou, "The Dove and the Darkness," pp. 277-279.
41. See Lewis, *Ecstatic Religion*.
42. John Keats, "Ode on a Grecian Urn," line 10, stanza V.
43. Jung, "Schiller's Ideas on the Type Problem, *Psychological Types*, CW 6.
44. Keats, "Ode on a Grecian Urn," lines 1-5, stanza V.
45. Thomas Mann, "Nietzsche's Philosophy in the Light of Recent History," *Last Essays*, p. 141.
46. Jung, *Psychological Types*, CW 6, pars. 484-488.
47. Joseph L. Henderson, "The Artist's Relation to the Unconscious," in *The Analytic Process*.
48. James Joyce, *Portrait of the Artist as a Young Man*, p. 213.
49. See Joseph Campbell and Henry Morton Robinson, *A Skeletal Key to Finnegan's Wake:* "The book is a kind of terminal moraine in which lie buried all the myths, programs, slogans, hopes, prayers, tools, educational theories, and theological bric-a-brac of the past millenium. And here, too, will be found the love that reanimates this debris. Joyce's moraine is not brickdust but humus; as he never tires of telling us, 'The same returns.'" (p. ix)
50. Richard Wilhelm, *The I Ching or Book of Changes*, p. 90.
51. Ibid., page 91, footnote.
52. Ibid, p. xxxii. (Jung's "Foreword to the I Ching" also appears in *Psychology and Religion: West and East*, CW 11.)
53. Percy Byshe Shelley, quoted by Joyce in *Portrait of the Artist as a Young Man*, p. 213.
54. Joseph Campbell, *The Masks of God: Creative Mythology*, pp. 67-69.
55. Jung, "The Apollonian and the Dionysian," *Psychological Types*, CW 6, par. 227.

56. Ibid., par. 230.
57. Ibid., par. 231.
58. Jung, "The Type Problem in Poetry," ibid., par. 323.
59. Ibid.
60. Henderson, "The Artists' Relation to the Unconscious."
61. Alfred North Whitehead, as reported by Lucien Price in *Conversations with Alfred North Whitehead* (not in print).
62. J.P. Eckermann, *Conversations with Goethe*, p. 83.
63. Jung, *Psychology and Religion*, CW 11, p. 358.
64. See F.M. Cornford, *From Religion to Philosophy*.
65. Jung, "The Type Problem in Classical and Medieval Thought," *Psychological Types*, CW 6.
66. See Marie-Louise von Franz, "Number Games of the Universe," and *Number and Time*.
67. See Erich Neumann, *The Origins and History of Consciousness*, pp. 102-103.
68. Marie-Louise von Franz, *Projection and Re-Collection in Jungian Psychology: Reflections of the Soul*, p. 66.
69. Ibid.
70. Von Franz, *Number and Time*, p. 154.
71. F.M. Cornford, *The Unwritten Philosophy and Other Essays*, p. 84.
72. Von Franz, *Number and Time*, p. 123.
73. Ibid.
74. Ibid.
75. Ibid., p. 124.
76. See James Hillman's criticism of Jung's views on the mandala as Self symbolism, implying that Jung presents the mandala as an image he consciously chose to feature as a symbol of monotheism ("Psychology: Monotheistic or Polytheistic?"). Actually, Jung discovered the significance of the mandala spontaneously in his own fantasies and in drawings of his patients. Hillman is right, however, in emphasizing the relativity of monotheism and polytheism, as I too have done here in the chapter on the religious attitude.
77. Von Franz, *Number and Time*, p. 131.
78. Joseph L. Henderson, "The Archetype of Culture."
79. Claude Lévi-Strauss, "The Scope of Anthropology," p. 11.
80. Ibid., pp. 13-16.
81. Ibid., p. 16.
82. Ibid.
83. Ibid., p. 17.

84. Williams, *Border Crossings*.

85. Lévi-Strauss, "Scope of Anthropology," p. HENDERSON.

86. Ibid., p. HENDERSON.

87. Ibid., p. HENDERSON.

88. Ibid., p. 43.

89. Jung, *Psychological Types*, CW 6, pars. 661-662.

90. Ibid., pars. 577-671.

91. Joan Evans, *Taste and Temperament*, pp. 30-44. Evans singles out two psychological functions which she calls *quick* and *slow* and sees them in a study of the visual arts, where each may display either an introverted or an extroverted style of composition. The quick style, which has decorative, levitational and experimental features, suggests the function of intuition. The slow style is earth-connected, contained, undramatic but totally real—in contrast to the imaginative flights of the quick style—and is therefore suggestive of the function of sensation. She cleverly points out how easily we may recognize these patterns not only in the visual arts but in the way people dress and furnish their homes, and I have noticed them myself in preferences people show for similar styles in architecture and gardening.

92. See Henderson, *Thresholds of Initiation*, pp. 53-57, for an interpretation of the dream. The amplification is the appendix, "The Bear as Archetypal Image."

93. Mircea Eliade, *Images and Symbols: Studies in Religious Symbols*, pp. 45-51.

94. Jung, *Psychology and Alchemy*, CW 12, par. 247.

95. Erich Neumann, "Mystical Man," in *The Mystic Vision*, p. 391.

96. Ibid., pp. 407-408.

97. Cornford, *Principium Sapientiae*, pp. 65-66.

98. Ibid., p. 74.

99. Ibid., p. 75.

100. Ibid.

101. Ibid., pp. 76-77.

102. Ibid., p. 78.

103. Ibid., p. 116.

104. Ibid., p. 118.

105. Ibid, p. 121..

106. Ibid.

107. Ibid.

108. Ibid.

109. Ibid, p. 148.

110. Jung, *Psychological Types*, CW 6, pars. 40-95.

111. This is elaborated in Jung's seminal essay, "The Transcendent Function," *The Structure and Dynamics of the Psyche*, CW 8.

112. Gerhard Adler, *Remembering and Forgetting*.

113. Ibid., p. 7.

114. Ibid., p. 15.

115. Ibid.

116. Von Franz, *Projection and Re-Collection*, p. 190.

117. Gerhard Adler and Aniela Jaffé, eds., *C.G. Jung Letters*, vol. 2, p. 539; see also Jung, *Mysterium Coniunctionis*, CW 14, par. 662.

118. Jung, "Synchronicity: An Acausal Connecting Principle," *The Structure and Dynamics of the Psyche*, CW 8, par. 870.

119. Von Franz, *Projection and Re-Collection*, p. 190.

120. Ibid., p. 195.

121. Von Franz, *Number and Time*, p. 283.

122. Ibid., p. 124.

123. See Jung, "On the Nature of the Psyche," *The Structure and Dynamics of the Human Psyche*, CW 8. Concerning the complementarity between physical and psychic events, Jung writes: "We are concerned first and foremost to establish certain analogies, and no more than that; the existence of such analogies does not entitle us to conclude that the connection is already proven. ...The existing analogies, however, are significant enough in themselves to warrant the prominence we have given them." (par. 442)

124. Anthony Stevens, *Archetypes: A Natural History of the Self*, p. 88.

125. Ibid., p. 89.

126. Ibid. (from Jung, "Foreword to Harding's *Woman's Mysteries*," *The Symbolic Life*, CW 18, par. 1229).

127. Ibid., p. 90.

128. Ibid., p. 91.

129. Ibid.

130. Ibid., pp. 91-96.

131. Erik Erikson, *Identity and the Life Cycle*, pp. 55-65.

132. Stevens, *Archetypes*, pp. 158-164.

133. Edward Edinger, "Romeo and Juliet: A Coniunctio Drama," in *The Shaman from Elko*.

134. Elizabeth Osterman, "The Tendency toward Patterning and Order in Matter and in the Psyche," in *The Reality of the Psyche*, pp. 24-25.

Glossary of Jungian Terms

Anima (Latin, "soul"). The unconscious, feminine side of a man's personality. She is personified in dreams by images of women ranging from prostitute and seductress to spiritual guide (Wisdom). She is the eros principle, hence a man's anima development is reflected in how he relates to women. Identification with the anima can appear as moodiness, effeminacy, and oversensitivity. Jung calls the anima *the archetype of life itself.*

Animus (Latin, "spirit"). The unconscious, masculine side of a woman's personality. He personifies the logos principle. Identification with the animus can cause a woman to become rigid, opinionated, and argumentative. More positively, he is the inner man who acts as a bridge between the woman's ego and her own creative resources in the unconscious.

Archetypes. Irrepresentable in themselves, but their effects appear in consciousness as the archetypal images and ideas. These are universal patterns or motifs which come from the collective unconscious and are the basic content of religions, mythologies, legends, and fairytales. They emerge in individuals through dreams and visions.

Association. A spontaneous flow of interconnected thoughts and images around a specific idea, determined by unconscious connections.

Complex. An emotionally charged group of ideas or images. At the "center" of a complex is an archetype or archetypal image.

Constellate. Whenever there is a strong emotional reaction to a person or a situation, a complex has been constellated (activated).

Ego. The central complex in the field of consciousness. A strong ego can relate objectively to activated contents of the unconscious (i.e., other complexes), rather than identifying with them, which appears as a state of possession.

Feeling. One of the four psychic functions. It is a rational function which evaluates the worth of relationships and situations. Feeling must be distinguished from emotion, which is due to an activated complex.

Individuation. The conscious realization of one's unique psychological reality, including both strengths and limitations. It leads to the experience of the Self as the regulating center of the psyche.

Inflation. A state in which one has an unrealistically high or low (negative inflation) sense of identity. It indicates a regression of consciousness into unconsciousness, which typically happens when the ego takes too many unconscious contents upon itself and loses the faculty of discrimination.

Intuition. One of the four psychic functions. It is the irrational function which tells us the possibilities inherent in the present. In contrast to sensation (the function which perceives immediate reality through the physical senses) intuition perceives via the unconscious, e.g., flashes of insight of unknown origin.

113

Participation mystique. A term derived from the anthropologist Lévy-Bruhl, denoting a primitive, psychological connection with objects, or between persons, resulting in a strong unconscious bond.

Persona (Latin, "actor's mask"). One's social role, derived from the expectations of society and early training. A strong ego relates to the outside world through a flexible persona; identification with a specific persona (doctor, scholar, artist, etc.) inhibits psycı ˙logical development.

Projection. The process whereby an unconscious quality or characteristic of one's own is perceived and reacted to in an outer object or person. Projection of the anima or animus onto a real women or man is experienced as falling in love. Frustrated expectations indicate the need to withdraw projections, in order to relate to the reality of other people.

Puer aeternus (Latin, "eternal youth"). Indicates a certain type of man who remains too long in adolescent psychology, generally associated with a strong unconscious attachment to the mother (actual or symbolic). Positive traits are spontaneity and openness to change. His female counterpart is the **puella,** an "eternal girl" with a corresponding attachment to the father-world.

Self. The archetype of wholeness and the regulating center of the personality. It is experienced as a transpersonal power which transcends the ego, e.g., God.

Senex (Latin, "old man"). Associated with attitudes that come with advancing age. Negatively, this can mean cynicism, rigidity and extreme conservatism; positive traits are responsibility, orderliness and self-discipline. A well-balanced personality functions appropriately within the puer-senex polarity.

Shadow. An unconscious part of the personality characterized by traits and attitudes, whether negative or positive, which the conscious ego tends to reject or ignore. It is personified in dreams by persons of the same sex as the dreamer. Consciously assimilating one's shadow usually results in an increase of energy.

Symbol. The best possible expression for something essentially unknown. Symbolic thinking is non-linear, right-brain oriented; it is complementary to logical, linear, left-brain thinking.

Transcendent function. The reconciling "third" which emerges from the unconscious (in the form of a symbol or a new attitude) after the conflicting opposites have been consciously differentiated, and the tension between them held.

Transference and countertransference. Particular cases of projection, commonly used to describe the unconscious, emotional bonds that arise between two persons in an analytic or therapeutic relationship.

Uroboros. The mythical snake or dragon that eats its own tail. It is a symbol both for individuation as a self-contained, circular process, and for narcissistic self-absorption.

Bibliography

Adler, Gerhard. *Remembering and Forgetting*. Privately printed in England, 1979.

Adler, Gerhard and Aniela Jaffé. *C.G. Jung Letters* (Bollingen Series XCV). 2 vols. Princeton University Press, Princeton, 1973-75.

Blake, William. *Poetry and Prose*. Ed. David Erdman. Doubleday, Garden City, 1965.

Boehme, Jakob. *The Works of Jacob Behemen*. 4 vols. Ed. G. Ward and T. Langcake. London, 1764-65.

Bowlby, John. *Attachment and Loss*. 2 vols. Hogarth Press and Institute of Psychoanalysis, London, 1969-73.

Campbell, Joseph. *The Masks of God: Creative Mythology*. Viking Press, New York, 1968.

Campbell, Joseph and Robinson, Henry Morton. *A Skeletal Key to Finnegan's Wake*. Viking Press, New York, 1944.

Castaneda, Carlos. *The Teachings of Don Juan: A Yaqui Way of Knowledge*. University Press, Berkeley, 1968.

Clark, Kenneth. *Civilisation: A Personal View*. Harper and Row, New York, 1970.

Cornford, F.M. *From Religion to Philosophy*. Arnold, London, 1912.

_____. *The Unwritten Philosophy and Other Essays*. Cambridge University Press, Cambridge, Mass., 1950.

_____. *Principium Sapientiae, A Study of the Origins of Greek Philosophical Thought*. Cambridge University Press, Cambridge, Mass., 1952.

Daniélou, Jean. "The Dove and the Darkness in Ancient Byzantine Mysticism." In *Man and Transformation* (Bollingen Series XXX). Eranos, vol. 5. Ed. Joseph Campbell. Pantheon, New York, 1964.

_____. "The Word Goes Forth, Christianity as a Missionary Religion." In *The Crucible of Christianity*. Ed. Arnold Toynbee. Thames and Hudson, London, 1969.

Dante Alighieri. *The Divine Comedy*. Trans. Lawrence Grant White. Pantheon, New York, 1948.

De Chardin, Teilhard. *Building the Earth*. Avon Books, New York, 1965.

Dourley, John P. *The Illness That We Are: A Jungian Critique of Christianity*. Inner City Books, Toronto, 1984.

Eckermann, J.P. *Conversations with Goethe*. George Bell and Sons, London, 1892.

Edinger, Edward. *Ego and Archetype: Individuation and the Religious Function of the Psyche.* G.P. Putnam's Sons for the C.G. Jung Foundation for Analytical Psychology, New York, 1972.

_____. *The Creation of Consciousness: Jung's Myth for Modern Man.* Inner City Books, Toronto, 1984.

_____. "Romeo and Juliet: A Coniunctio Drama." In *The Shaman from Elko: Papers in Honor of Joseph L. Henderson on His Seventy-Fifth Birthday.* C.G. Jung Institute, San Francisco, 1978.

Edman, Irwin. *Four Ways of Philosophy.* Henry Holt, New York, 1937.

Eliade, Mircea. *Images and Symbols: Studies in Religious Symbols.* Trans. Philip Mairet. Sheed and Ward, New York, 1961.

_____. *Shamanism: Archaic Techniques of Ecstasy* (Bollingen Series LXXVI). Trans. Willard R. Trask. Princeton University Press, Princeton, 1964.

_____. *The Myth of the Eternal Return.* (Bollingen Series XLVI). Trans. Willard R. Trask. Pantheon Books, New York, 1954.

Eliot, T.S. *The Wasteland and Other Poems.* Harcourt, Brace, New York, 1930.

_____. *Collected Poems 1909-35.* Harcourt, Brace, New York, 1936.

_____. *The Family Reunion.* Harcourt, Brace, New York, 1939.

Erikson, Erik. *Identity and the Life Cycle.* W.W. Norton, New York, 1980.

Evans, Joan. *Taste and Temperament.* Macmillan, New York, 1939.

Evdokimov, Paul. *La Femme et le Salut Du Monde: Ètude D'Anthropologie Christienne sur les Charismes de la Femme.* Casterman, Paris, 1958.

Henderson, Joseph L. "The Artist's Relation to the Unconscious." In *The Analytic Process.* International Congress for Analytical Psychology, Zurich. G.P. Putnam's Sons for the C.G. Jung Foundation for Analytical Psychology, New York, 1971.

_____. *Thresholds of Initiation.* Wesleyan University Press, Middletown, Conn., 1967.

_____. "The Archetype of Culture." In *The Archetype.* Ed. A. Guggenbühl-Craig. Karger, New York, 1964.

_____. "Ancient Myths and Modern Man." In *Man and His Symbols.* Ed. C.G. Jung. Doubleday, New York, 1964.

Henderson, Joseph L. and Oakes, Maud. *The Wisdom of the Serpent.* George Braziller, New York, 1963.

Hesse, Herman. *The Glassbead Game: Magister Ludi.* Trans. Mervyn Savill. Frederick Ungar, New York, 1949.

Hillman, James. "Psychology: Monotheism or Polytheism?" In *Spring 1971*.

Hobbes, Thomas. *Leviathan, or the Matter, Forme and Power of A Commonwealth Ecclesiasticall and Civil.* London, 1651. Printed for Andrew Crooke.

Jaffé, Aniela. *From the Life and Work of C.G. Jung.* Harper Colophon Books, New York, 1971.

_____. *The Myth of Meaning in the Works of C.G. Jung.* Trans. R.F.C. Hull. Hodder and Stoughton, London, 1970.

James, William. *Pragmatism: A New Name For Some Old Ways of Thinking.* Longmans, Green, New York, 1931.

Joyce, James. *Portrait of the Artist as a Young Man.* Viking Press, New York, 1964.

_____. *Finnegan's Wake.* Viking Press, New York, 1943.

_____. *Ulysses.* Sylvia Beach, Paris, 1923.

Jung, C.G. *The Collected Works* (Bollingen Series XX). 20 vols. Trans. R.F.C. Hull. Ed. H. Read, M. Fordham, G. Adler, Wm. McGuire. Princeton University Press, Princeton, 1953-1979.

Keats, John. *Collected Poems.* Oxford University Press, New York, 1956.

Lévi-Strauss, Claude. "The Scope of Anthropology." Inaugural lecture, Chair of Social Anthropology, Collège de France, Paris, 1960. Jonathan Cape, London, 1967.

Lewis, I.M. *Ecstatic Religion: An Anthropological Study of Spirit Possession and Shamanism.* Penguin Books, London, 1971.

Mann, Thomas. "Nietzsche's Philosophy in the Light of Recent History." In *Last Essays*. Secker and Warburg, London, 1959.

_____. *The Magic Mountain.* Alfred A. Knopf, New York, 1939.

Mieklejohn, Alexander. *Education Between Two Worlds.* Harper, New York, 1942.

Neumann, Erich. *Art and the Creative Unconscious* (Bollingen Series XLI). Trans. Ralph Manheim. Princeton University Press, Princeton, 1959.

_____. *The Archetypal World of Henry Moore.* Trans. R.F.C. Hull. Pantheon, New York, 1959.

_____. "Mystical Man." in *The Mystic Vision* (Bollingen Series XXX). Eranos, vol. 6. Ed. Joseph Campbell. Princeton University Press, Princeton, 1968.

_____. *The Origins and History of Consciousness* (Bollingen Series XLII). Trans. R.F.C. Hull. Pantheon Press, New York, 1954.

Osterman, Elizabeth. "The Tendency toward Patterning and Order in Matter and in the Psyche." In *The Reality of the Psyche*. Ed. Joseph B. Wheelwright. G.P. Putnam's Sons for the C.G. Jung Foundation for Analytical Psychology, New York, 1968.

Paracelsus, Theophiastus Bombustes of Hokenheim. *De Vita Longa*. Ed. Adam von Bodenstein, Basel, 1562.

Proust, Marcel. *Remembrance of Things Past*. Trans. C.K. Scott-Moncrief. Henry Holt, New York, 1924.

Raine, Kathleen. *Blake and Tradition* (Bollingen Series XXXV). Princeton University Press, Princeton, 1968.

Read, Herbert. *Icon and Idea*. Harvard University Press, Cambridge, Mass., 1965.

_____. *The Green Child*. New Directions, New York, 1935.

Schiller, J.C.F. von. *On the Aesthetic Education of Man, in a Series of Letters*. Trans. Reginald Snell. New Haven and London, 1954.

Schwartz-Salant, Nathan. *Narcissism and Character Transformation: The Psychology of Narcissistic Character Disorders*. Inner City Books, Toronto, 1982.

Sharp, Daryl. *The Secret Raven. Conflict and Transformation*. Inner City Books, Toronto, 1980.

Stevens, Anthony. *Archetypes: A Natural History of the Self*. William Morrow, New York, 1982.

Tillich, Paul. "The Importance of New Being for Christian Theology." In *Man and Transformation* (Bollingen Series XXX). Eranos, vol. 5. Ed. Joseph Campbell. Pantheon, New York, 1964.

Turner, Victor. *The Ritual Process, Structure and Anti-Structure*. Aldine Publishing Co., Chicago, 1969.

_____. *The Forest of Symbols, Aspects of Modern Ndembu Ritual*. Cornell University Press, Ithaca, N.Y., 1967.

Von Franz, Marie-Louise. *Projection and Re-Collection in Jungian Psychology: Reflections of the Soul*. Open Court, LaSalle, Ill., 1980.

_____. *Number and Time*. Trans. Andrea Dykes. Northwestern University Press, Evanston, Ill., 1974.

_____. "Number Games of the Universe." Lecture delivered at the Second Bailey Island Conference, Brunswick College, Brunswick, Maine, 1971.

_____. *The Problem of the Puer Aeternus*. Sigo Press, Santa Monica, 1981.

_____. "The Process of Individuation." In *Man and His Symbols*. Ed. C.G. Jung. Doubleday, New York, 1964.

Waley, Arthur. *The Way and Its Power.* Grove Press, New York, 1958.

Whyte, Lancelot Law. *The Next Development in Man.* Henry Holt, New York, 1948.

_____. *The Unconscious Before Freud.* Basic Books, New York, 1960.

Wilhelm, Richard. *The I Ching or Book of Changes* (Bollingen Series XIX). Trans. Cary F. Baynes. Pantheon, New York, 1950.

Williams, Donald Lee. *Border Crossings: A Psychological Perspective on Carlos Castaneda's Path of Knowledge.* Inner City Books, Toronto, 1981.

Wolff, Toni. "Structural Forms of the Collective Psyche." G.H. Graber, Bern, Switzerland, 1956.

Woodman, Marion. *Addiction to Perfection: The Still Unravished Bride.* Inner City Books, Toronto, 1982.

Woolf, Virginia. *Mrs. Dalloway.* Hogarth Press, London, 1929.

Yates, Frances. *Giordano Bruno and the Hermetic Tradition.* London, 1964.

Index

Abraxas, 33
absolute knowledge, 95-96
active imagination, 52-56, 61-66, 70, 83, 103-106
Addiction to Perfection, 51
Adler, Alfred, 34
Adler, Gerhard, 94
aesthetic arrest, 50
aesthetic attitude, 9, 11-14, 23, 25-27, 45-58, 72-78
air, as god-image, 35-38
alchemy, 30-33
amplification, 55, 81
analysis/analytic process, 7-14, 17-22, 24-25, 27-30, 35-44, 51-56, 59-67, 82-86, 94-97, 99-106
analytical psychology, 7-14, 51-56, 83-87, 93-99
anima, 36
animus, 54-55
"Answer to Job," 59
anthropology, 72-75, 77-78
Anthropos, 22-24, 53
Apollo/Apollonian, 52-53, 88, 91
archetype(s)/archetypal image(s), 11, 22-23, 29-32, 34-44, 56-57, 64-71, 81-87, 92, 95-106
Aristotle, 67, 77, 93
art, and religion, 56
Art for Art's Sake, 46-49, 54
Art of the Mind, 18
asceticism, 39-44
Athena, 29
Attachment and Loss, 98
attitude(s), cultural: aesthetic, 9, 11-14, 23, 25-27, 45-48, 72-78
  identification with, 7-8, 11-12, 17-18, 21-22, 27, 83

philosophic, 9, 11-14, 19, 21, 23, 25, 45, 49, 59-78
psychological, 7-14 and *passim*
religious, 11-14, 19, 23, 26-44, 49, 72-78
scientific, 72, 76-77
social, 8-9, 11-14, 17-27, 45, 49, 53, 58, 66, 72-78
and typology, 75-77
and vocation, 76
axis mundi, 82

baptism, 38
bear, in dream, 81
Black Madonna, 58
Blake, William, 31
Boehme, Jacob, 31
Bowlby, John, 98
Buddha/Buddhism, 36, 42-43

Campbell, Joseph, 48, 50
Castaneda, Carlos, 74
cave, in dream, 40
centering, psychic, 82-86, 96-97, 103-106
Christ, 33, 38, 43, 108-109
Christianity, 31-44, 46-48, 74, 101
Churchill, Winston, 25
Cimabue, 58
Civilisation, 46, 49
Clark, Kenneth, 46, 49
compensation, 8, 20, 34-35, 44
complex, mother, 99-101
Confucius, 50
Cornford, F.M., 67, 88-92
Cosmic Man, 24, 107-108
countertransference, 11-14
creation myth, 62-66
creativity, 46-47, 52-57, 61-66, 88-92

cultural attitudes, *see* attitudes,
     cultural

Daniélou, Jean, 38
Dante, 34, 37, 102
Darwin, 42
death, and rebirth, 29-32, 86, 106
deflation, psychic, 34, 37
Democritus, 67, 88
Descartes, 77
Dionysus/Dionysian, 33, 52-53,
     89
Divine Child, 57-58
Divine Comedy, The, 34
Dorn, Gerhard, 31
dove, wings of, 29, 39, 43-44
dream(s): amplification of, 55, 81
     of bear, 81
     of cave, 40
     centering images in, 82-83
     drawing of temple in, 30
     of egg, 40
     and free association, 54-55
     god-images in, 29-30, 33-34
     of steps, 30
     of trickster-figure, 54-55
     of vegetable garden, 8, 19-20
     wind in, 35, 38
     of works of art, 54-55
Durkheim, 72-73

earth/earthy, 39-42, 62-65, 105-
     106
Edinger, Edward, 28, 102
Edman, Irwin, 72
education theories, 25-26, 76
ego-consciousness, 11, 27, 35,
     83-84, 94
Einstein, 42
Eliade, Mircea, 30, 82
Eliot, T.S., 27, 48-49
Empedocles, 90
Epicurus, 89

Erikson, Erik, 101
Eros, 21, 24
eternal recurrence, 30, 86
ethology, 98-99
Evans, Joan, 76
existential analysis, 7
extraversion, 9, 60

feeling (function), 20-21, 75
feminine, importance of, 20, 34
femme inspiratrice, 36
Finnegan's Wake, 47-48
fire, 29, 38
Flaubert, 9
Four Ways of Philosophy, 72
France, Anatole, 9
free association, 53
Freudian psychology, 7-8, 10-11,
     27, 53, 72, 85, 93-94
functions, psychological, *see*
     typology

Gaia, 29
Galileo, 42
Gandhi, 25
Giotto, 58
glass, 50-51
Glass Bead Game, The, 7-8
god-image, in dreams, 29-30, 33-
     34
Goethe, 56, 90
grace, 50
grandiosity, 34
Greek mythology/religion, 29, 59
Green Child, The, 21

Harrison, Jane, 29
Heisenberg, 65
Hephaestos, 29
Heraclitus, 90, 92
hermaphrodite, 29
Hermes, 29
hero-image, 35, 84

Hesiod, 91
Hesse, Herman, 7
Hippocrates, 91
Hobbes, Thomas, 21-23
Holy Spirit, 35-39
Homer, 29, 88-89, 91
Human Potential Movement, 7
humanism, 74
hysteria, 37

I Ching, 50
identity, with cultural attitude, 7-
     8, 11-12, 17-18, 21-22, 27,
     83
Imitatio Christi, 43
individualism, 18-20, 23-24
individuation, 7-8, 18-20, 23-24,
     44, 54-56, 83, 86, 97
inferiority complex, 34
Inferno, 102
inflation, psychic, 23, 34-35, 37
initiation, 27-28, 30, 38, 77-78,
     81, 84-85, 89, 102, 106
initiation hunger, 102, 106
inspired madness, 88-91
introversion, 19, 52, 60, 75, 87,
     93
intuition (function), 19, 55, 60,
     75, 88, 111

Jacobi, Jolande, 104
Jaffé, Aniela, 32
James, William, 10
Joyce, James, 47-49
Judaism, 39
Jung, C.G., 8-11, 13, 22, 32-34,
     45-46, 48, 50-54, 59-62, 70,
     72, 75, 81-86, 93-99

kairos, 28, 31, 33
Kali, 100-101
Kandinsky, 49
Keats, John, 45

Kerényi, C., 29
King, Martin Luther, 25
Klee, Paul, 49

Lafayette, Mme de, 9
Leonardo da Vinci, 69, 77
Leviathan, 16, 21-22
Lévi-Strauss, Claude, 72-75
Lewis, I.M., 37, 43
light of nature, 32-33, 39, 44
Lincoln, Abraham, 25
Lipps-Worringer hypothesis, 46
Logos, 24, 28, 66
love, 102-106
lumen naturae, 32-33, 39, 44

madness, inspired, 88-91
magic flight, 43, 85, 90
mandala, 67, 82, 110
Mann, Thomas, 46, 48-49
mantic inspiration, 88-89
Maria Prophetissa, axiom of, 69
mathematics, 65
Mauss, 72-73
Meiklejohn, Alexander, 26, 76
Mercurius duplex, 32-33
Merleau-Ponty, 75
Middle Ages, 46, 49, 93
monotheism, 29-30, 42-44
Moore, Henry, 57
mother complex, 99-101
mother-child relationship, 98-102
Musaeum hermeticum, 31
Muses, 89
mysticism, 28, 30-34, 38-39, 43-
     44, 86-87, 90-91

narcissism, 18
natural philosophy, 59-61
Neo-Platonism, 31, 42-43
Neumann, Erich, 9, 86-87, 96
Newton, 42
Next Development in Man, The, 94

Nietzsche, 46, 52-53
nominalism, 61, 93-95
number symbolism, 30, 62-70,
    95-97

object relations, 99
opposites, 31-34, 53, 59, 61, 63-
    64, 85, 97, 102-106
ordered sequence, of archetypes,
    66
Orpheus/Orphic, 33, 42, 91
Osterman, Elizabeth, 103
Ovid, 29

Paracelsus, 31-32, 39
Pareminides, 90
Pentecost, 38-39
personality functions, *see* typology
philosophic attitude, 9, 11-14, 19,
    21, 23, 25, 45, 49, 72-78
Plato/Platonic, 21, 36, 43, 67, 91,
    93-94
poet-philosopher, 88-92
polytheism, 29-30, 34
*Portrait of the Artist as a Young
    Man*, 47-48
Poseidon, 29
pragmatism, 10, 73
primal Self, 84-86, 97, 99
Principium Sapientiae, 88
projection(s), 12, 36, 92, 101
Proust, Marcel, 9, 47
psyche, reality of, 13, 24
Psychological Types, 93
puer aeternus, 34-36
Pythagoras, 89

quintessentia, 69-70

rationalism, 10
Read, Sir Herbert, 21
realism, 61, 93-95
rebirth, 30-31, 41-44, 83

reductive analysis, 85-86
religion, and art, 56
religious attitude, 11-14, 19, 23,
    26-44, 49, 72-78
religious conversion, 27
Remembrance of Things Past, 47
Renaissance, 46, 57, 74
Republic, 21
resistance, to analysis, 51-53, 60
resurrection, 30-31, 83
Robinson, Henry, 48
Rochefoucauld, Duc de la, 9
Romanticism, 45-46, 52
Romeo and Juliet, 102
Roosevelt, Franklin, 25
Rose Garden, 30
rose window, 80, 82
Rousseau, Jean Jacques, 25-26
Royce, Josiah, 10

Saint-Simon, Duc de, 9
Satan, 34
Schiller, 45, 53
Schopenhauer, 46
science, 42, 50, 52, 65, 73, 76-
    77, 94
scientific attitude, 50, 72, 76-77
"Scope of Anthropology, The," 72
seer, 88-92
Self (archetype), 27, 57, 70, 83-
    87, 94-97, 99, 109
semiology, 73
sensation (function), 55, 60, 75,
    111
Sévigné, Mme de, 9
shadow, 34
shamanism, 42-43, 88-92
Sharp, Daryl, 13
Shekinah, 36
Shelley, Percy Byshe, 50
Sholem, Gershom, 59
social attitude, 8-9, 11-14, 17-27,
    45, 49, 53, 58, 66, 72-78

Socrates, 50, 88, 91
Sophia, 36
source mysticism, 86-87, 96
spirit, and nature, 64-65
spiritualism, 37
Stendhal, 9
Stephens, Anthony, 98-99, 102
steps, in dream, 30
surrealism, 49
symbol, reconciling/unifying, 53-
    56, 61, 82-86
Symbols of Transformation, 81
synchronicity, 62, 95-97

t'ai chi symbol, 62
Tao/Taoism, 62, 97
Tara, 36
Taste and Temperament, 76
Teachings of Don Juan, The, 74
Teilhard de Chardin, 42
Tellus Mater, 58
temple, in dream, 30
theology, 28, 42-44
theos, 28-29
Thresholds of Initiation, 83
thinking (function), 60, 75
Tillich, Paul, 28
Timaeus, 91
transcendentalism, 30-31, 33-34,
    42-44
transference, 11-14, 51-52, 84, 95
trickster-figure, 35, 55, 84
Turner, Victor, 17, 22

typology, 50, 60, 72, 75-77, 93,
    111

ultimate Self, 84-86, 97
Ulysses, 48
unconscious, discovery of, 93-94
Unconscious Before Freud, The,
    93
unus mundus, 70
uroboros, 86-87, 96
utopian systems, 21

Virgin, Black, 58
Virgin Mary, 38, 56-57, 101
Voltaire, 21, 59
von Franz, Marie-Louise, 24, 65-
    67, 69-70, 94-95, 97

water, 29, 38
Weltanschauung, 8-14, 25
Whyte, L.L., 93-94
Williams, Donald Lee, 74
wind, in dream, 35, 38
wings, 29, 39, 43-44
Woodman, Marion, 51
Woolf, Virginia, 20

xenophobia, 17, 23

yin/yang, 62

Zeus, 29
Zola, Emile, 9

Addiction to Perfection
The Still Unravished Bride

A Psychological Study by
Marion Woodman

12. Addiction to Perfection: The Still Unravished Bride.
Marion Woodman (Toronto). ISBN 0-919123-11-2. 208 pages. $12

"This book is about taking the head off an evil witch." With these words Marion Woodman begins her spiral journey, a powerful and authoritative look at the psychology and attitudes of modern woman.

The witch is a Medusa or a Lady Macbeth, an archetypal pattern functioning autonomously in women, petrifying their spirit and inhibiting their development as free and creatively receptive individuals. Much of this, according to the author, is due to a cultural one-sidedness that favors patriarchal values—productivity, goal orientation, intellectual excellence, spiritual perfection, etc.—at the expense of more earthy, interpersonal values that have traditionally been recognized as the heart of the feminine.

Marion Woodman's first book, *The Owl Was a Baker's Daughter: Obesity, Anorexia Nervosa and the Repressed Feminine,* focused on the psychology of eating disorders and weight disturbances.

Here, with a broader perspective on the same general themes, Marion Woodman continues her remarkable exploration of women's mysteries through case material, dreams, literature and mythology, in food rituals, rape symbolism, Christianity, imagery in the body, sexuality, creativity and relationships.

The final chapter, a discussion of the psychological meaning of ravishment (as opposed to rape), celebrates the integration of body and spirit and shows what this can mean to a woman in terms of her personal independence.

Studies in Jungian Psychology
by Jungian Analysts

LIMITED EDITION PAPERBACKS

Prices quoted are in U.S. dollars (except for Canadian orders)

1. **The Secret Raven: Conflict and Transformation.**
   Daryl Sharp (Toronto). ISBN 0-919123-00-7. 128 pages. $10

A concise introduction to the application of Jungian psychology. Focuses on the creative personality – and the life and dreams of the writer Franz Kafka – but the psychology is relevant to anyone who has experienced a conflict between the spiritual life and sex, or between inner and outer reality. (Knowledge of Kafka is not necessary.) Illustrated. Bibliography.

2. **The Psychological Meaning of Redemption Motifs in Fairytales.**
   Marie-Louise von Franz (Zurich). ISBN 0-919123-01-5. 128 pages. $10

A unique account of the significance of fairytales for an understanding of the process of individuation, especially in terms of integrating animal nature and human nature. Particularly helpful for its symbolic, nonlinear approach to the meaning of typical dream motifs (bathing, beating, clothes, animals, etc.), and its clear description of complexes and projection.

3. **On Divination and Synchronicity: Psychology of Meaningful Chance.**
   Marie-Louise von Franz (Zurich). ISBN 0-919123-02-3. 128 pages. $10

A penetrating study of the meaning of the irrational. Examines time, number, and methods of divining fate such as the I Ching, astrology, Tarot, palmistry, random patterns, etc. Explains Jung's ideas on archetypes, projection, psychic energy and synchronicity, contrasting Western scientific attitudes with those of the Chinese and so-called primitives. Illustrated.

4. **The Owl Was a Baker's Daughter: Obesity, Anorexia Nervosa, and the Repressed Feminine.**
   Marion Woodman (Toronto). ISBN 0-919123-03-1. 144 pages. $10

A pioneer work in feminine psychology, with particular attention to the body as mirror of the psyche in eating disorders and weight disturbances. Explores the personal and cultural loss – and potential rediscovery – of the feminine principle, through Jung's Association Experiment, case studies, dreams, Christianity and mythology. Illustrated. Glossary. Bibliography.

5. **Alchemy: An Introduction to the Symbolism and the Psychology.**
   Marie-Louise von Franz (Zurich). ISBN 0-919123-04-X. 288 pages. $16

A lucid and practical guide to what the alchemists were really looking for – emotional balance and wholeness. Completely demystifies the subject. An important work, invaluable for an understanding of images and motifs in modern dreams and drawings, and indispensable for anyone interested in relationships and communication between the sexes. 84 Illustrations.

6. **Descent to the Goddess: A Way of Initiation for Women.**
   Sylvia Brinton Perera (New York). ISBN 0-919123-05-8. 112 pages. $10

A timely and provocative study of women's freedom and the need for an inner, female authority in a masculine-oriented society. Based on the Sumerian goddess Inanna-Ishtar's journey to the underworld, her transformation through contact with her dark "sister" Ereshkigal, and her return. Rich in insights from dreams, mythology and analysis. Glossary. Bibliography.

7. **The Psyche as Sacrament: C.G. Jung and Paul Tillich.**
   John P. Dourley (Ottawa). ISBN 0-919123-06-6. 128 pages. $10

An illuminating, comparative study showing with great clarity that in the depths of the soul the psychological task and the religious task are one. With a dual perspective, the author—Jungian analyst and Catholic priest—examines the deeper meaning, for Christian and non-Christian alike, of God, Christ, the Spirit, the Trinity, morality and the religious life. Glossary.

8. **Border Crossings: Carlos Castaneda's Path of Knowledge.**
   Donald Lee Williams (Boulder). ISBN 0-919123-07-4. 160 pages. $12

The first thorough psychological examination of the popular don Juan novels. Using dreams, fairytales, and mythic and cultural parallels, the author brings Castaneda's spiritual journey down to earth, in terms of everyone's search for self-realization. Special attention to the psychology of women. (Familiarity with the novels is not necessary.) Glossary.

9. **Narcissism and Character Transformation: The Psychology of Narcissistic Character Disorders.**
   Nathan Schwartz-Salant (New York). ISBN 0-919123-08-2. 192 pp. $13

An incisive and comprehensive analysis of narcissism: what it looks like, what it means and how to deal with it. Shows how an understanding of the archetypal patterns that underlie the individual, clinical symptoms of narcissism can point the way to a healthy restructuring of the personality. Draws upon a variety of psychoanalytic points of view (Jungian, Freudian, Kohutian, Kleinian, etc.). Illustrated. Glossary. Bibliography.

10. **Rape and Ritual: A Psychological Study.**
    Bradley A. Te Paske (Minneapolis). ISBN 0-919123-09-0. 160 pp. $12

An absorbing combination of theory, clinical material, dreams and mythology, penetrating far beyond the actual deed to the impersonal, archetypal background of sexual assault. Special attention to male ambivalence toward women and the psychological significance of rape dreams and fantasies. Illustrated. Glossary. Bibliography.

11. **Alcoholism and Women: The Background and the Psychology.**
    Jan Bauer (Zurich). ISBN 0-919123-10-4. 144 pages. $12

A major contribution to an understanding of alcoholism, particularly in women. Compares and contrasts medical and psychological models, illustrates the relative merits of Alcoholics Anonymous and individual therapy, and presents new ways of looking at the problem based on case material, dreams and archetypal patterns. Glossary. Bibliography.

12. **Addiction to Perfection: The Still Unravished Bride.**
    Marion Woodman (Toronto). ISBN 0-919123-11-2. 208 pages. $12

A powerful and authoritative look at the psychology and attitudes of modern woman, expanding on the themes introduced in *The Owl Was a Baker's Daughter*. Explores the nature of the feminine through case material, dreams and mythology, in food rituals, rape symbolism, perfectionism, imagery in the body, sexuality and creativity. Illustrated.

13. **Jungian Dream Interpretation: A Handbook of Theory and Practice.**
    James A. Hall, M.D. (Dallas). ISBN 0-919123-12-0. 128 pages. $12

A comprehensive and practical guide to an understanding of dreams in light of the basic concepts of Jungian psychology. Jung's model of the psyche is described and discussed, with many clinical examples. Particular attention to common dream motifs, and how dreams are related to the stage of life and individuation process of the dreamer. Glossary.

14. **The Creation of Consciousness: Jung's Myth for Modern Man.**
Edward F. Edinger, M.D. (Los Angeles). ISBN 0-919123-13-9. 128 pages. $12

An important new book by the author of *Ego and Archetype,* proposing a new world-view based on a creative collaboration between the scientific pursuit of knowledge and the religious search for meaning. Explores the significance for mankind of Jung's life and work; discusses the purpose of human life and what it means to be conscious; examines the theological and psychological implications of Jung's master-work, *Answer to Job;* presents a radical, psychological understanding of God's "continuing incarnation"; and illustrates the pressing need for man to become more conscious of his dark, destructive side as well as his creative potential. Illustrated.

15. **The Analytic Encounter: Transference and Human Relationship.**
Mario Jacoby (Zurich). ISBN 0-919123-14-7. 128 pages. $12

A sensitive and revealing study that differentiates relationships based on projection from those characterized by psychological distance and mutual respect. Examines the psychodynamics activated in any intimate relationship, and particularly in therapy and analysis; summarizes the views of Jung and Freud on identification, projection and transference-countertransference, as well as those of Martin Buber (I-It and I-Thou relationships); and shows how unconscious complexes may appear in dreams and emotional reactions. Special attention to the so-called narcissistic transferences (mirror, idealizing, etc.), the archetypal roots of projection and the significance of erotic love in the analytic situation. Glossary. Bibliography.

16. **Change of Life: A Psychological Study of the Menopause.**
Ann Mankowitz (Santa Fe). ISBN 0-919123-15-5. 128 pages. $12

A detailed and profoundly moving account of a menopausal woman's Jungian analysis, openly facing the fears and apprehensions behind the collective "conspiracy of silence" that surrounds this crucial period of every woman's life. Dramatically interweaves the experience of one woman with more generally applicable social, biological, emotional and psychological factors; frankly discusses the realities of aging, within which the menopause is seen as a potentially creative rite of passage; and illustrates how the menopause may manifest, both in outer life and in dreams, as a time of rebirth, an opportunity for psychological integration and growth, increased strength and wisdom. Glossary. Bibliography.

All books contain detailed Index

INNER CITY BOOKS
Box 1271, Station Q, Toronto, Canada M4T 2P4
(416) 927-0355